The Dragonflies & Damselflies of Cheshire

Richard Gabb & David Kitching

NATIONAL MUSEUMS & GALLERIES
· ON MERSEYSIDE ·

British Library Cataloguing-in-Publication
Data Available

© Board of Trustees of the National Museums &
Galleries on Merseyside

First published in Great Britain 1992

ISBN 0 906367 54 9

Contents

Foreword 5

Acknowledgements 7

Chapter one
Introduction 9

Chapter two
Recording History: pre 1985 12

Chapter three
The Tetrad (2 kilometre) Breeding Survey 1985-1991 15

Chapter four
Status, Distribution & Field Notes 18

Chapter five
Habitats & Prime Sites 51

References 62

FOREWORD

Dragonflies and damselflies are beautiful and enthralling insects, and Cheshire is a favoured county with twenty-five certainly recorded species of which nineteen are known to breed. They grace the meres and mosses, marl pits, ponds and rivers which provide such a rich diversity of freshwater habitats in the county, and a summer day in a watery place not enlivened by dragonflies is hard to imagine. However, now as perhaps never before in their three hundred million year history, dragonflies face serious threats to their survival. Being dependent upon water in which to pass their larval lives, they are extremely vulnerable to loss of habitat as a result of drainage and pollution. Richard Gabb and David Kitching highlight several instances where man's activities in Cheshire have had an apparently deleterious effect upon dragonflies, although on the other hand, examples of enrichment to the fauna have also been detected.

To enable us to monitor any future population changes in our local dragonflies, a reliable database on their current status is needed, and this is provided most excellently by this book. The authors have processed over 5,800 records, old and new, from the literature, from their own work and, very importantly, from submissions by a long list of contributors to the Ten Kilometre Square Recording Scheme (1979-1984), with Ian Rutherford as county recorder, and to its successor, the Tetrad Breeding Survey organised by Richard Gabb. This represents an enormous amount of work and deserves our warmest thanks and congratulations.

But the task, as the authors clearly state, is by no means complete. This has to be an ongoing exercise and " exciting discoveries certainly await those prepared to continue the fieldwork ". This book must stimulate and encourage further observation of the dragonflies of Cheshire; by so doing it will achieve the success it most certainly merits.

R.R. Askew
18.12.91

DEDICATION

For Sonia Holland whose initial comments led to the development of the Cheshire Tetrad Breeding Survey and whose subsequent interest provided us with continuing encouragement.

ACKNOWLEDGEMENTS

Whilst it is customary to express thanks to those who have provided particular support we must emphasise that this book could not have been written without considerable help from the following:

Dr Richard Askew for acting as referee and so kindly writing the foreword. Tony Broome for drawing the prime site location maps. Cheshire Scout Council for allowing us access to key sites on their land in Delamere. English Nature for grant aid towards fieldwork, and in particular Colin Hayes for his encouragement and advice. Brian Eversham of the Biological Records Centre at the Institute of Terrestrial Ecology for access to records. Grosvenor Museum, Chester for access to their collection and historic records. Stephen Hind for his manual mapping and exceptional levels of field recording. Lancashire and Cheshire Entomological Society for funding the Annual Reports. Robert Letsche for the photograph of the Hairy Dragonfly (*Brachytron pratense*). Manchester Museum for access to their collection and entomological literature. National Museums and Galleries on Merseyside for access to their collections and historic records, and in particular Stephen Judd who brought the whole project through the several years of production, funding, review and promotion with a drive and enthusiasm which must be an example to other museums. Also to Phil Phillips for computer work and Val Evans the designer. Robert Merritt, the National Recorder during much of the Tetrad Scheme for his initiatives. Ken Ogden for so discretely improving the original grammar. Barbara Porter for her assistance with botanical recording at the prime sites. Ian Rutherford for his years of directing the 10 Kilometre Recording Scheme and for making relevant personal correspondence available. Dr Alan Savage for providing much data on the biology of key Cheshire sites. Chris Shields whose superb illustrations have enhanced the book beyond expectations. Philip Smith for the photograph of the Club-tailed Dragonfly (*Gomphus vulgatissimus*). Warrington Museum and Alan Leigh for access to their collections and records.

To the landowners who, almost without exception, have given us permission to explore sites on their property.

Most importantly to all those who have contributed records since 1980, namely: Phillipa Adams, K.Allenby, Richard Askew, Peter Atherton, Rodney Baguley, Michael Bailey, Gordon Bennett, Stuart Bertenshaw, Anthony Blackledge, Sheila Blamire, Richard Blindell, Anthony Broome, D.Burn, M.Carter, Gary Cleland, P.Dalgleish, Ken Darwin, J.Davidson, John Daws, Roger Dennis, Brian Dickson, Richard Doran, Susan Doran, Steven Edwards, Dennis Elphick, Richard Gabb, Phillip Garnett, A.Gradwell, William Gradwell, F.Grayson, Paul Griffiths, Jonathan Guest, Les Hall, Ian Hesketh, Harry Hind, Stephen Hind, Paul Hughes, Alan Hunter, A.de Hutiray, R.Jackson, David Jeffers, Stephen Judd, Scott Kennedy, D.Kingham, David Kitching, Shirley Kitching, Thomas Kitching, Henry Larsen, Robert Letsche, D.Lewis, Tom Mawdsley, Robert Merritt, Julie Molyneux, Celia Muir, John Oxenham, N.Pacey, Antony Parker, Michael Passant, L.Passey, J.Phillips, Jonathan Pickup, Barry Poole, John Rayner, Alan Roberts, Roger Robinson, Charles Russell, Ian Rutherford, Alan Savage, Elizabeth Seddon, John Seddon, Barry Shaw, Peter Shaw, Brian Smith, J.Smith, Len Smith, Philip Smith, Darwyn Sumner, Gillian Taylor, Michael Taylor, S.Taylor, Lee Thickett, David Thompson, J.Thompson, Michael Tilling, Brian Walker, Tom Wall, Brenda Wallace, Ian Wallace, Patrick Waring, Robert Whitehead, Elyse Wilson, David Wright, Crawford Young, Simon Young, and of course, our apologies to anyone we have forgotten.

AUTHORS

Richard Gabb developed the concept of the Tetrad Breeding Survey for Cheshire dragonflies which, after ten years, has culminated in this book. He is a keen photographer and a past committee member of the British Dragonfly Society. Like many others, Richard's first passion was ornithology; he is on the committee of the Cheshire and Wirral Ornithological Society and edits their quarterly newsletter. Richard is currently the Managing Director of a manufacturing stationery company in Manchester.

David Kitching has worked for Cheshire County Council's Countryside Management Service since 1979 and is now Countryside Manager responsible for Ranger services in the eastern half of Cheshire. His fascination with dragonflies and their behaviour developed after he discovered the Broad-bodied Chaser breeding in a disused railway cutting when he was working on the development of the Middlewood Way near Macclesfield in the early 1980's. The collation of the dragonfly survey data provided an opportunity to combine dragonfly research with an interest in computing and led to the development of programmes which were used to analyse the data for this book.

Chapter one
Introduction

"it may perhaps be stated as a fact, that a greater surface of land is covered in water in Cheshire, than in any other county in England ...."
HENRY HOLLAND (1808)

Cheshire is a beautiful area of England although we might be expected to say that having walked through most parts of the county in our search for dragonflies. Geography textbooks portray Cheshire as an area of intensive dairy farming and this is an impression which is likely to be confirmed in the minds of those who pass through the county along the M6 motorway. Driving north, a few may glance across to the Pennine hills and wonder about the 'ruins' of Mow Cop which show up so prominently on the skyline. Travelling in the opposite direction even fewer people are likely to notice the Welsh mountains away to the west. The area between is termed the Cheshire and Shropshire Plain and although this is the dominant feature when viewed from the eastern hills the county is a lot more varied than first appears. Looking out from Tegg's Nose, some 350 metres above sea level, several outcrops of hills will be seen on a clear day. The nearest of these at Alderley Edge are not prominent but the Peckforton range stands out as part of the mid-Cheshire ridge which runs from Frodsham to Bickerton. From this vantage point on exceptional days the Welsh mountains can be seen in the far distance, whilst further still to the south the Wrekin and the Long Mynd occasionally appear some 74 and 100 kilometres away respectively. Cheshire is also crossed by several rivers and their tributaries, all of which flow towards the north and west. These, together with several canals and many still quiet villages, form a mosaic of what can be described as classic English countryside.

The sheer abundance and diversity of different water bodies in the county, as described by Henry Holland in the opening quotation, may still be found today. Their significance for dragonfly populations is substantial and at least one nationally important species occurs here in greater numbers than in most other English counties. Cheshire has indeed proved to be an exciting county for dragonflies during the renaissance in recording, which has taken place over the last few years throughout the new county and the whole of the Wirral.

Geology

The geology of the county and the effects of the last ice-age are two of the most important factors determining the distribution of dragonflies in Cheshire. The ice-sheet moved down from the north and covered much of the county until its retreat between 12,000 and 14,000 years ago. Consequently all the species to be found today must have re-colonised since this time. As the life cycle of a dragonfly is largely associated with water it is the influence of this ice sheet upon the topography and the formation of water bodies, together with the type of underlying rock, that has determined much of the present day dragonfly habitat in the county.

Some 300 million years ago the whole region was covered by sea with deposits of mud and sand which over a long period became compressed to form the underlying bed-rock. The Pennine hills in the east of Cheshire are predominantly composed of sandstones and shales. Both types of rock give rise to acidic soils which influence the water chemistry of the Pennine edge ponds and consequently attract dragonfly species preferring such water.

Moving out into the Plain the bedrock is also sandstone but this time laid down in the Triassic period. The outcropping hills at Alderley Edge, the mid-Cheshire ridge and higher parts of the Wirral are all composed of this Triassic sandstone. Soils associated with the sandstone are also thin and acidic, giving rise to heathland which supports particular dragonfly habitats and species.

Certain parts of the lowland Plain are covered by Keuper Marls which lie over the upper layers of sandstone from which they take their name. These marls provided a natural fertilising effect when spread on the land and thus led to the digging of thousands of small pits in the fields of Cheshire. Their subsequent filling with water has created another very important dragonfly habitat.

Over countless years deposits of rock salt dissolved away naturally leading to the creation of large underground voids. These subsequently collapsed, so creating key dragonfly sites today. Such natural subsidence is one origin of a number of the Cheshire meres, although more recently the pumping of natural brine has also caused subsidence and the formation of shallow lakes and pools known as 'flashes'.

Extraction of boulder clay, sand and gravel has affected areas of heathland in Cheshire but has in turn left further waters for the benefit of dragonflies. The clay has been used for brick making and the disused water-filled clay pits have now become another excellent dragonfly habitat.

The debris carried by the ice sheet was deposited to form undulating mounds known as moraine, so helping to shape the course of today's streams and rivers which provide a further specialised habitat for dragonflies. The size and movement of all these types of water, their chemistry and associated vegetation, the mean temperatures and the mobility of particular species are important issues determining the variety of dragonfly to be found in Cheshire. Together with the much more immediate and rapid effects of drainage and pollution, these factors have influenced both the numbers and the diversity of species during the relatively short period of recent recording.

Cheshire Dragonfly List

39 species of dragonfly currently breed in Great Britain and Ireland and a further 2 species can be regarded as regular immigrants to the south of England. 25 species from the British list have been proven to occur in Cheshire with a further 4 having been recorded by individuals without independent confirmation. Of these 25 species only the 2 immigrants have not been observed during the period of the 10 Kilometre and Tetrad Recording Schemes from 1978 to 1989. 19 species are known to breed in the county and the other 2 must certainly do so although the larvae, emergence or exuviae have not yet been observed.

The Cheshire species recorded to date are listed below:

DRAGONFLIES (Anisoptera)

OCCURRENCES SINCE 1980

1 SOUTHERN HAWKER
   Aeshna cyanea
2 COMMON HAWKER
   Aeshna juncea
3 BROWN HAWKER
   Aeshna grandis
4 EMPEROR DRAGONFLY
   Anax imperator
5 HAIRY DRAGONFLY
   Brachytron pratense
6 CLUB-TAILED DRAGONFLY
   Gomphus vulgatissimus
7 DOWNY EMERALD
   Cordulia aenea
8 KEELED SKIMMER
   Orthetrum coerulescens
9 BROAD-BODIED CHASER
   Libellula depressa
10 FOUR-SPOTTED CHASER
   Libellula quadrimaculata
11 WHITE-FACED DARTER
   Leucorrhinia dubia
12 BLACK DARTER
   Sympetrum danae
13 RUDDY DARTER
   Sympetrum sanguineum
14 COMMON DARTER
   Sympetrum striolatum

OCCURRENCES BEFORE 1980

15 YELLOW-WINGED DARTER
   Sympetrum flaveolum
16 RED-VEINED DARTER
   Sympetrum fonscolombei

UNCORROBORATED RECORDS

17 GOLDEN-RINGED DRAGONFLY
   Cordulegaster boltonii
18 BLACK-TAILED SKIMMER
   Orthetrum cancellatum
19 SCARCE CHASER
   Libellula fulva

DAMSELFLIES (Zygoptera)

OCCURRENCES SINCE 1980

20	BANDED DEMOISELLE	
	Calopteryx splendens	
21	BEAUTIFUL DEMOISELLE	
	Calopteryx virgo	
22	EMERALD DAMSELFLY	
	Lestes sponsa	
23	RED-EYED DAMSELFLY	
	Erythromma najas	
24	LARGE RED DAMSELFLY	
	Pyrrhosoma nymphula	
25	BLUE-TAILED DAMSELFLY	
	Ischnura elegans	
26	COMMON BLUE DAMSELFLY	
	Enallagma cyathigerum	
27	AZURE DAMSELFLY	
	Coenagrion puella	
28	VARIABLE DAMSELFLY	
	Coenagrion pulchellum	

UNCORROBORATED RECORD

29	SCARCE BLUE-TAILED DAMSELFLY	
	Ischnura pumilio	

In the British context certain Cheshire species are of particular significance. The White-faced Darter (*Leucorrhinia dubia*) is undoubtedly the most important due to its relative abundance in the Delamere area. No area further south supports anything like the numbers found here and even many more northerly sites have smaller populations, which is all the more reason to protect the acid mosslands. A surprising discovery has been the Club-tailed Dragonfly (*Gomphus vulgatissimus*) on the River Dee and considering the limited numbers seen even on its stronghold rivers such as the Thames, Severn and Wye this must be a significant extension of its known breeding range. Two further species warrant mention in a national context. The Variable Damselfly (*Coenagrion pulchellum*) and the Hairy Dragonfly (*Brachytron pratense*) are declining nationally, the latter due to habitat loss and the former for reasons not yet understood. Both are to be found in Cheshire with numbers of the Hairy Dragonfly apparently increasing and more sites for the Variable Damselfly undoubtedly awaiting discovery. Whilst infrequent arrivals of casual species such as the Keeled Skimmer (*Orthetrum coerulescens*) are of little significance, the recent arrival and breeding of the Ruddy Darter (*Sympetrum sanguineum*) and the probable breeding of the Emperor Dragonfly (*Anax imperator*) suggest significant extensions to their normal ranges.

The abundance of diverse habitats in Cheshire clearly provides a distinct advantage over adjacent counties. Certain species however are bordering on their northerly limit in Cheshire and occur more commonly further south. Perhaps a continuing series of mild winters and fine summers will allow the Migrant Hawker (*Aeshna mixta*) to continue to move north and colonise the county. Permanent breeding populations of the Emperor Dragonfly should also become established and even the enigmatic Golden-ringed Dragonfly (*Cordulegaster boltonii*) may arrive from the Derbyshire or Clwyd breeding colonies. Exciting discoveries certainly await those prepared to continue the fieldwork.

CHAPTER TWO
RECORDING HISTORY: PRE 1985

"One afternoon in July, just as the sun was getting near the horizon and I was facing west for home, I came across numbers of L. quadrimaculata resting on the tops of the heather......... There they were, at varying intervals, with their wings spread out and glistening, for all the world like distant windows in the setting sun. Far away, for a long distance on the heath, I could easily make them out."
JOHN ARKLE (1898)

I first read the above description of dragonflies on the Delamere heathland several years ago during research into historic records for the county. Even now, each time I visit the area, Arkle's comments bring to mind a picture of dragonflies occurring in great abundance. The Delamere mosses remain one of the best sites in Cheshire to find relatively high numbers, despite an undoubted reduction in the size and the quality of this habitat over the last century. Whilst a fair proportion of the historic records refer to sites which cannot be precisely located today, the value of such information is considerable, and particularly so when described in such an evocative way. Our research has encompassed the specimen collections and record cards at Chester, Liverpool, Manchester and Warrington Museums, together with the collation of records from regional and national journals. Darwyn Sumner, the Lancashire County Recorder, has provided much further information and Brian Eversham of the Biological Records Centre at Monks Wood kindly made available all their records. From these sources we have been able to summarise some 400 species records between the late 1800's and 1977 when C.I.Rutherford began to organise systematic recording within the 10 kilometre Ordnance Survey grid. Whilst this represents a considerable increase in information compared to that available to Ian Rutherford, it must still only represent part of the picture and any further records would be welcomed by the authors.

The Early Years 1875-1930

The earliest record we have is that of the Red-eyed Damselfly (*Erythromma najas*) made at Pettypool by B.Cooke in 1875. About this time he was noting the Beautiful Demoiselle (*Calopteryx virgo*) on the River Dee although this species has not been recorded on the river since. Cooke (1882) also has the distinction of producing the first known list of dragonflies for Lancashire and Cheshire. J.Arkle, who lived in Chester, must have been an enthusiastic collector and recorder, often being quoted by W.J.Lucas who was acting as National Recorder and who became the author of the first definitive book on British dragonflies in 1900. Arkle, whose collection is housed in the Grosvenor Museum, Chester, can be attributed with two 'first records for Cheshire'; the migrant Red-veined Darter (*Sympetrum fonscolombei*) in 1890, and the Keeled Skimmer (*Orthetrum coerulescens*) in 1898, both at Oakmere. Neither species has been recorded more than a few times in the county since then. His 1898 paper on dragonflies is well worth reading, not least for its delightful style. How topical his comments seem, viewed almost one hundred years later, when he describes an apparent decline in numbers of the Large Red Damselfly (*Pyrrhosoma nymphula*), then listed as *Pyrrhosoma minimum*.

"The localities had changed during the last few years. They were drier, - the Scotch firs and birches

had grown up, overshadowing the ground, and P. minimum had disappeared....... let an insect's habitat be transformed, - for example, if a marsh, let it be drained, - and the place thereof shall know it no more."

Over the early years of the new century up to 1920 such names as G.A.Dunlop, W.Tattershall, C.R.Brown and the illustrious T.A.Coward, whose reputation in ornithology and writings about Cheshire are so well known, were all contributing records. These were being published annually by W.J.Lucas in the proceedings of the Lancashire and Cheshire Fauna Committee. W.J.Lucas, a London schoolteacher, is one of the major figures in the history of British odonatology, and we should regard ourselves as fortunate that he also acted as Vice-President of the Lancashire and Cheshire Entomological Society between 1909 and 1911. Lucas (1919) summarised the Odonata of Lancashire and Cheshire (together with Denbigh and Westmorland) listing some 20 species including the still enigmatic Golden-ringed Dragonfly (*Cordulegaster boltonii*). He regarded our region as being on the borderline between northern and southern species of dragonfly and speculated upon the future discovery of species such as the Brilliant Emerald (*Somatochlora metallica*) due to it being found further south, and even the Northern Damselfly (*Coenagrion hastulatum*). Some 26 recorders were acknowledged as forwarding specimens or notes for the paper. Lucas continued to publish Cheshire records throughout the 1920's, with Dr A.Randall Jackson making significant contributions which included the possible sighting of a pair of Hairy Dragonflies (*Brachytron pratense*) in a lane near Chester in 1921. A further summary of all Cheshire species was made by Lucas in a checklist of the fauna of Lancashire and Cheshire in 1930. This listed 22 species including the Hairy Dragonfly which was subsequently confirmed in Cheshire in 1934.

Mid Century Recording 1930-1977

H.Burrows, W.K.Ford and in particular H.Britten, made major contributions to the study of Cheshire dragonflies between 1930 and 1960. Britten was Assistant Keeper of Entomology at Manchester Museum between 1911 and 1936, and President of the Lancashire and Cheshire Fauna Committee (1931-1933) for which he was Cheshire Dragonfly Recorder (1932-1936). Dragonfly records for these three decades were predominantly made by Burrows and Britten. From a rarity standpoint they found the immigrant Darters in 1941 and 1945 and Britten confirmed the presence of the Hairy Dragonfly (*Brachytron pratense*) at Pulford in 1934, and again at Hatchmere in 1943. Yet the paucity of records of the more common species at many sites over the years underlined the message preached by Lucas, and still true today, that all records are useful.

The third member of the trio, W.K.Ford, was Keeper of Invertebrate Zoology at Liverpool Museum. He, together with Britten, took over the mantle of Lucas in summarising the Odonata records for the Lancashire and Cheshire Fauna Committee during the 1940's and 50's. Of note in this period were several references to the Variable Damselfly (*Coenagrion pulchellum*) which was still to be seen at such places as Upton and Meols on the Wirral. For the first time the name of Cynthia Longfield is found as a contributor of records and as an adjudicator of specimens whilst based at the Natural History Museum (then, British Museum of Natural History).

A further milestone was passed in 1953 when Ford reviewed the known Odonata records for Lancashire and Cheshire. He listed some 23 species as having occurred in Cheshire and for the first time there was speculation upon the future discovery of the Emperor Dragonfly (*Anax imperator*) and the Migrant Hawker (*Aeshna mixta*). It is perhaps pertinent here to refer specifically to a few of his comments. He felt it necessary to point out that there were so few records of proof of breeding that it would be useful to record nymphs, nymphal skins (exuviae) and oviposition in order to distinguish between resident species and casual visitors. He also remarked upon the process of urbanisation and changed agricultural operations making it pointless to search for some species at localities quoted in the last century. His paper essentially summarises and re-states information previously mentioned. An update, covering further records which came to light as a result of his 1953 paper, was published in 1954. In this paper Ford refers to a female specimen of that extremely rare migrant, the Vagrant Darter (*Sympetrum vulgatum*), in Arkle's collection. However, after critical examination by Cynthia Longfield, the identification was later corrected to the Red-veined Darter (*Sympetrum fonscolombei*).

The 1960's and early 1970's were a period of casual recording with much of the information being collected by the Lancashire County Recorder.

The 10 Kilometre Recording Scheme 1978-1984

There had been a considerable increase of interest in Odonata since the publication of C.O.Hammond's The Dragonflies of Great Britain and Ireland in 1977. In the same year David Chelmick was appointed National Dragonfly Recorder. The national scheme asked for sightings to be recorded within the 10 kilometre squares of the Ordnance Survey grid. At this time the Cheshire County Recorder for Lepidoptera was Ian Rutherford and he agreed to co-ordinate dragonfly recording in addition to his work on the butterflies and moths. Ian has kindly made available to us his annual statements on records received for the years between 1978 and 1984, together with any relevant personal correspondence. At the start of the 10 Kilometre Square Recording Scheme it is interesting to read that there were just four people living in the county who were thought to be active recorders. The post 1960 database was made available to Ian and listed 17 species having been recorded from the 30 full or part 10km squares which made up the old county of Cheshire.

Records during this period included:- The Four-spotted Chaser (*Libellula quadrimaculata*), the Downy Emerald (*Cordulia aenea*) and the Banded Demoiselle (*Calopteryx splendens*) being recorded in 1978 for the first time since 1960. A second site was found in 1979. By 1980 the Emerald Damselfly (*Lestes sponsa*) was being found more widely in the County and 1981 saw the first modern record for the Beautiful Demoiselle (*Calopteryx virgo*).

In 1982 Ian issued a matrix of species to 10 kilometre squares showing some 231 records with a maximum of 14 different species in any one square. Subsequent notable records included the finding of the Downy Emerald (*Cordulia aenea*) in 1983, by R.Merritt, the National Recording Scheme Organiser, in a second 10 kilometre square (SJ56) at Shemmy Moss; the almost simultaneous first modern recording of the Variable Damselfly (*Coenagrion pulchellum*) by S.Judd and B.Walker at Hatchmere and the sighting of a solitary male Keeled Skimmer (*Orthetrum coerulescens*) by C.Young at Risley Moss.

It is important to commend Ian Rutherford's efforts during these years in generating enthusiasm for dragonfly recording at a time when he was also doing the same for the butterflies and moths.

CHAPTER THREE
THE TETRAD (2 KILOMETRE) BREEDING SURVEY 1985-1991

"I think there is great potential in Cheshire as it all appears to be rather under-recorded"
DAVID CHELMICK,
NATIONAL ODONATA
RECORDER, JULY 1977

Background

Ian Rutherford found that he had insufficient time to deal with the Odonata in the depth that he wished and consequently he transferred responsibility to myself (Richard Gabb) in 1985. The challenge of photographing such beautiful but wary insects had attracted me for some time and during occasional return visits to my home county of Gloucestershire I looked for species such as the Club-tailed Dragonfly (*Gomphus vulgatissimus*) and the Ruddy Darter (*Sympetrum sanguineum*), neither of which was then known to occur in Cheshire. With a need for careful stalking the behaviour of a dragonfly photographer is likely to attract attention and a group of bird ringers, finding me photographing in their 'patch', suggested that I should contact Sonia Holland, the Gloucestershire recorder. Our subsequent meeting proved invaluable and led to my changing the recording scheme in Cheshire from a 10 kilometre to a 2 kilometre square basis.

Up to this time I had accepted the limited usefulness of simply noting the presence of dragonflies within a 10 kilometre area, realising that vagrant species passing through the county provided records that were interesting but hardly significant. I therefore wondered if a change to recording within the smaller squares could be linked to a better understanding of those species which were breeding and where this was occurring in the county. Such an increase in information would make a much more significant contribution to our knowledge.

The 10 Kilometre Recording Scheme had covered all the "old" county of Cheshire which included the "pan handle" in the north east. This area was removed from Cheshire after local government reorganisation in 1974 as was a large part of the Wirral, whilst parts of Warrington and Widnes were added. After some thought it was decided to adopt the new county boundary for the tetrad survey but to include the Wirral which is not physically connected to any other county. This definition of Cheshire is identical to that used in the earlier tetrad breeding bird survey. Having designed the new recording scheme it was necessary to promote it and to attract an increasing number of recorders. Liverpool Museum supported the development work and indeed have been one of the main agents for encouraging interest over recent years in this and other areas of entomology. They proved very helpful in promoting the new scheme by arranging meetings which enabled potential recorders to understand the scheme's requirements and to examine specimens of adult dragonflies and exuviae. During the first year of the tetrad scheme Stephen Hind processed all the record forms and updated the tetrad dot maps by hand. It was soon clear that the volume of information being submitted was such that a computer programme was needed which would both print the record in the correct tetrad square and designate symbols for the different levels of possible, probable and proven breeding.

Recording Data - The Cheshire Dragonfly Recording Form

A site recording card was designed and distributed to stimulate submission of records and to standardise data retrieval. Recorder and species information was supported by data on location, habitat and behaviour.

This was provided by the recorder filling in requested information or ticking a box against a listed character if the information was positive. The following data categories were employed.

RECORDER AND SPECIES INFORMATION
    Recorder's name
    Date of record
    Species recorded at site
    Stage: nymph/exuviae/teneral/adult
    Sex
    Numbers present

LOCATION INFORMATION
    Site name
    Six figure National Grid reference
    Tetrad designation: normally filled in by scheme organisers. A tetrad is a 2 kilometre X 2 kilometre square formed by the even numbered kilometre grid lines, with 25 tetrads comprising one 10 kilometre square. Each tetrad is designated by a letter.

E	J	P	U	Z
D	I	N	T	Y
C	H	M	S	X
B	G	L	R	W
A	F	K	Q	V

HABITAT INFORMATION
This was optional but most recorders responded.
    Water body type: lake/pond/ditch/stream/river/canal/ marsh/bog, with a box to cover sites where species were seen away from water.
    Water body condition: running/still/clear/muddy/algae cover/polluted/fished
    pH value
    Aspect: open/part shade/enclosed
    Vegetation: aquatic/emergent/adjacent
    Other comments

BEHAVIOUR
    Territorial/display/copulation/oviposition

The recording of the developmental stage and behaviour of the insects marked a step forward, as this was the first time that such data had been included in a county survey of Odonata. With a mobile species it is important to differentiate between casual observations which have little significance to the status of the insect within the locality and the records which indicate a breeding population.

A simple observation which might include an insect defending a territory, was taken to indicate only the possibility of a breeding population, whilst copulation or ovipositing indicates probable successful breeding. The recording of nymphs or exuviae is positive proof of breeding and can indicate the most important sites for each species.

Distribution Maps

Data from the record cards were transferred onto an Acorn Archimedes computer by D.Kitching. Using the database as the core to the development of a suite of menu driven programmes it was possible to link information to the production of tetrad dot maps and histograms which show the flight period for each species. The production of dot maps using interactive software was unique in county dragonfly recording schemes and this has made both data handling and the identification of under-recorded areas or key sites considerably easier than the normal manual methods used by recorders. Another very useful feature relating to the flexibility of the system is that, when linked to a second processor, it has been possible to transfer the records from our database direct to the database held on the mainframe computer at Monks Wood Biological Records Centre. This is achieved by simply sending a floppy disc through the post. The saving in input time for the staff at Monks Wood has been considerable and this facility has also avoided the transposing of data from the Cheshire records onto National Recording Cards. It is also possible to transfer the data direct to the recording package 'Recorder' which has been developed by English Nature (formerly the Nature Conservancy Council). Five map symbols were adopted denoting the three levels of observed breeding status, pre-tetrad scheme records, and recent uncorroborated records of species not previously seen in Cheshire. The symbols used are:

- ● Proven breeding: exuviae or nymphs recorded
- • Probable breeding: insects observed copulating or ovipositing
- · Possible breeding: insects seen but no breeding behaviour recorded
- ☐ Pre-1980 record
- ? Uncorroborated record: species new or scarce to Cheshire

Over the period of the tetrad scheme 95 recorders have submitted over 5000 species records to date. The total database is now 5805 records and the current number of species recorded in each tetrad is illustrated below. Those tetrads showing no records may contain no suitable habitat and this is certainly true for some of the empty Pennine edge squares and those surrounding major urban areas. The Wirral is under-recorded and there is much scope for increasing the number of species in many other tetrads. There is always a tendency to concentrate on the "hot spots" in the prime habitat areas and important discoveries will most likely favour those who are prepared to explore the lesser known regions.

All data are held at Liverpool Museum including computer printouts in both species and tetrad order. The results of the Tetrad Recording Scheme to the end of the 1991 season, illustrating the distribution of each species found in Cheshire, are discussed in the following chapter.

Number of species recorded in each tetrad during the survey period 1980-1991.

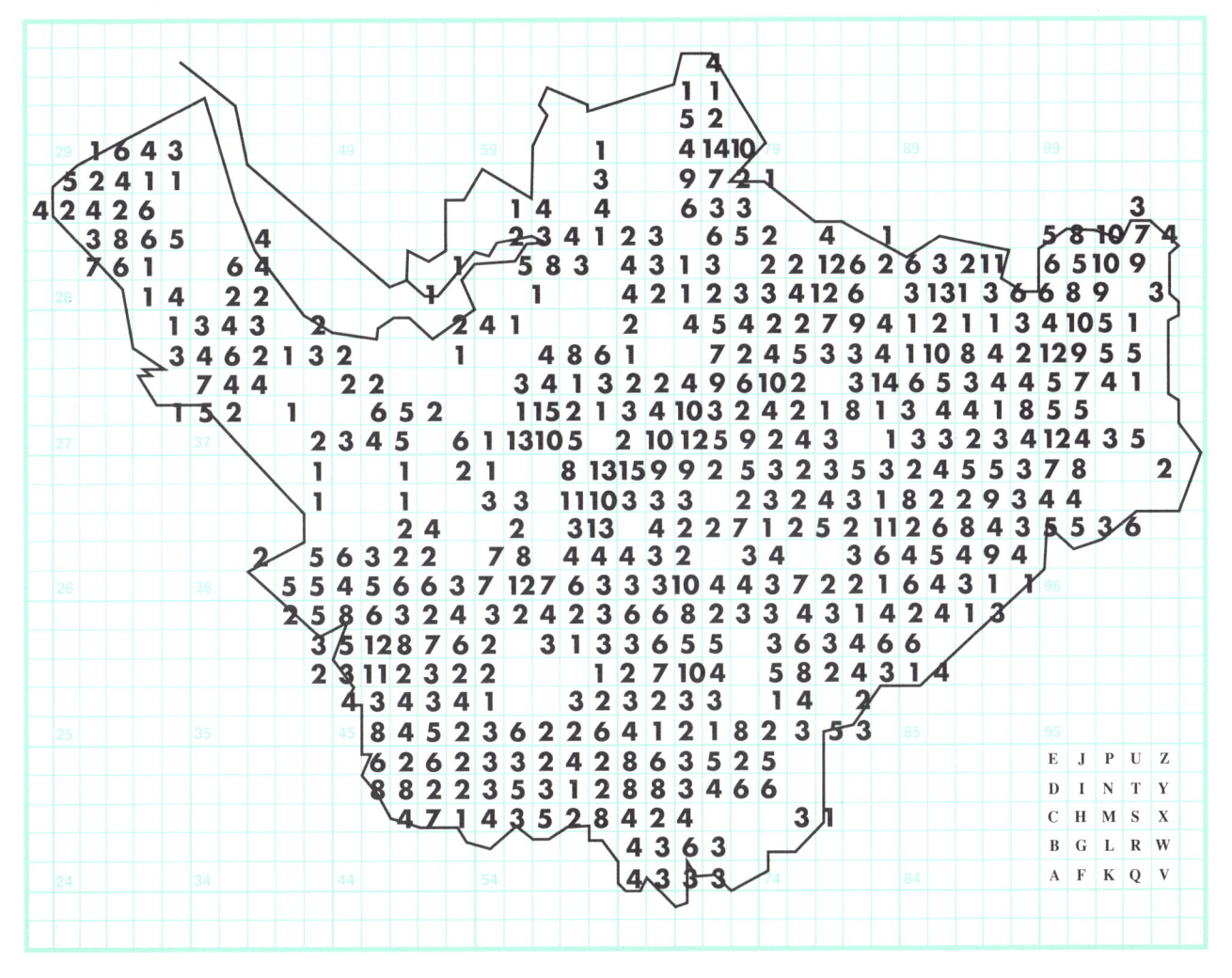

Chapter Four
Status, distribution & Field Notes

The information for each species is presented in this chapter under the following headings:-

1 Field Notes

Notes on the behaviour and occurrence of each species with comments on discrepancies between the Cheshire survey and other literature.

2 Cheshire status & distribution

A description of the status of each species in Cheshire with comments on some of the notable sites where they occur.

3 Flight period

A histogram based on the recorded data showing the flight period for each species in Cheshire.

4 Tetrad map

A map of Cheshire overlain with a tetrad grid with symbols to show breeding status.

5 Database

A statistical representation of the recorded distribution of each species according to breeding status.

SOUTHERN HAWKER
Aeshna cyanea
(Müller, 1764)

FIELD NOTES

The Southern Hawker may be first encountered when it comes to investigate the presence of the observer. It is certainly the most approachable of the Hawker species and often remains at rest for several minutes. Association with garden ponds makes the Southern Hawker one of the most noticeable species. Males tend to search for females by flying between two and three metres above the water. In comparison, the Common Hawker (*Aeshna juncea*) usually flies much lower when on territory. The Southern Hawker frequently lays eggs in a variety of inappropriate sites. Examples noticed in Cheshire are cracks in crazy paving, paths around ponds and into fissures in tree bark some distance from water. Ovipositing also commonly occurs into moss and old *Typha* stems at some height above water.

CHESHIRE STATUS AND DISTRIBUTION

The Southern Hawker uses a wide variety of breeding waters in Cheshire. These range from the smallest garden pond, through ditches and marl pits, to larger pools associated with the mosses. Existing literature appears somewhat contradictory in suggesting a specific association with either acidic or alkaline waters. This species can certainly be described as a coloniser of new sites irrespective of the pH value of the water. The apparently north-easterly distribution cannot solely be attributed to recording bias. The Southern Hawker is certainly scarcer in the central, southern and south-westerly tetrads with one full 10 kilometre square having no records. It is interesting to note that this tallies with the proportional distribution shown on the original 10km maps in Hammond (1977). Perhaps this species has some preference for waters which are grading towards the acidic rather than neutral. Sites where this species can be seen regularly are Lindow Common (88F), Danes Moss (97A) and Woolston Eyes (68P). Population density seems to be somewhat cyclic with a decline being noticed during the late 1980's in comparison to the earlier years of the present recording scheme.

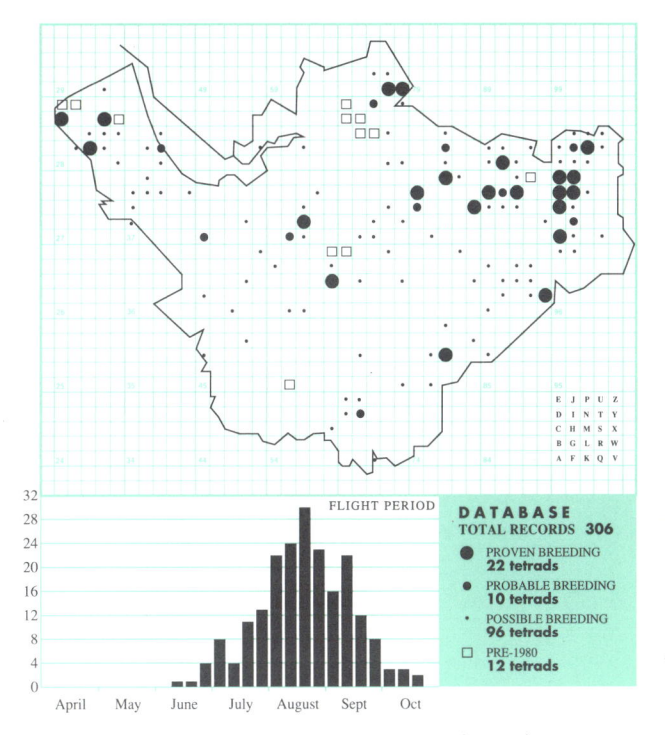

The earliest record to date is 15th June 1986 by P.Griffiths at Broomhall (64I) and the latest record is 17th October 1986 by M.Tilling at Delamere Forest (57K).

DATABASE
TOTAL RECORDS 306
- PROVEN BREEDING 22 tetrads
- PROBABLE BREEDING 10 tetrads
- POSSIBLE BREEDING 96 tetrads
- PRE-1980 12 tetrads

COMMON HAWKER
Aeshna juncea
(Linnaeus, 1758)

FIELD NOTES

In comparison with the Southern Hawker (*Aeshna cyanea*), the Common Hawker is mainly restricted to acidic waters. Once it has established its territory the Common Hawker flies endlessly backwards and forwards, frequently searching for females low down amongst the marginal vegetation. In Cheshire it can be confirmed as inhabiting woodland edges and rides, particularly on windy days. Given some sunshine there seems to be a willingness for this species to fly at lower temperatures. This dragonfly pays little attention to the observer and rarely settles for long. In Cheshire it has consistently been the first of the three Cheshire *Aeshna* species to emerge. Females frequently oviposit into submerged marginal vegetation deep in the rushes, only revealing their presence by the clattering of wings against the stems as they change position. Exuviae have mainly been found much lower down the stems of the rushes than is the case with other members of this family.

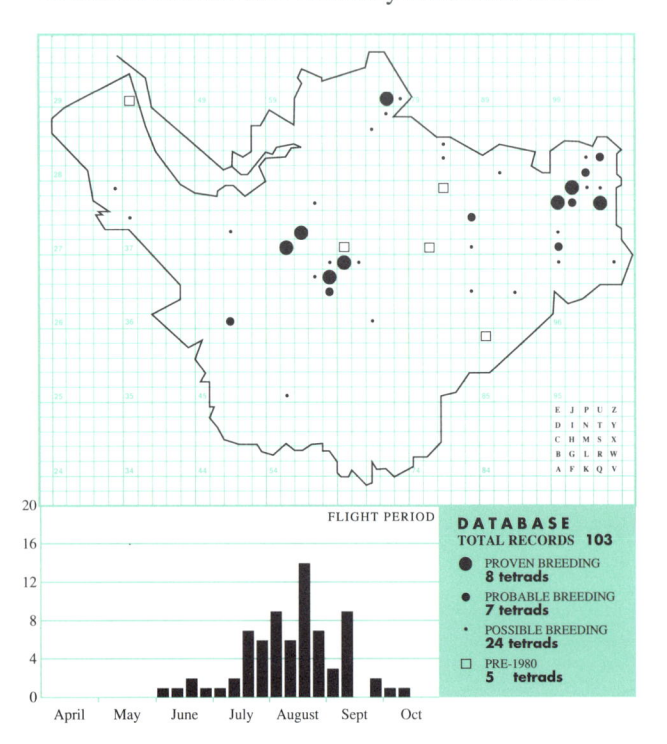

CHESHIRE STATUS AND DISTRIBUTION

The main populations of this species are associated with the natural ponds and probably the streams on the gritstone and coal measures in the east of the county lying within the Pennine foothills. One private artificial pond at Bollington (97D) has a large breeding population. This pond is adjacent to these natural sites but it is only marginally acidic although it does have a low level of dissolved nutrients in the water. Another nearby breeding site at Adlington is eutrophic and consequently supports much lower numbers. Substantial edge vegetation, consisting mainly of *Juncus* species, also seems a pre-requisite for breeding.

Moving westwards, each of the main clusters of records is associated with an acidic mossland. For example, Lower Moss Wood (77X), Risley Moss (69Q), Hatchmere (57L) and Gull Pool (56Z/66E) (part of the Abbots Moss complex). Other individual tetrad records away from these sites are probably vagrants. Nowhere within Cheshire is the Common Hawker a common dragonfly. The earliest record to date is 3rd June 1986 by D.Kitching at Bollington (97D) and the latest record is 10th October 1985 by G.Cleland near the River Weaver (57T).

DATABASE
TOTAL RECORDS 103
- PROVEN BREEDING 8 tetrads
- PROBABLE BREEDING 7 tetrads
- POSSIBLE BREEDING 24 tetrads
- PRE-1980 5 tetrads

BROWN HAWKER
Aeshna grandis
(Linnaeus, 1758)

FIELD NOTES

In comparison with other species there is a much greater likelihood of this particular Hawker being found flying in less than ideal conditions. On windy, cool and overcast days it may still be found feeding in the lee of hedgerows. In Cheshire it is not noticeably a woodland species, seeming to prefer fields and other open spaces. It may also be found in built-up areas. The Brown Hawker can be a wary dragonfly but it does seem to land frequently, albeit for relatively short periods. It very often rests in tall grasses. At breeding sites it flies higher than the other two Hawker species. On occasion it will fly late at dusk catching prey around street lamps.

CHESHIRE STATUS AND DISTRIBUTION

The Brown Hawker is said in some of the literature not to breed in acidic waters. This is untrue in Cheshire where a very broad spectrum of habitat is chosen. Some of the more acidic waters including the mosses do have populations of Brown Hawker breeding alongside species such as the Black Darter (*Sympetrum danae*) which is always associated with such habitat. Yet it is also found breeding in more neutral waters such as canals and marl pits. It requires emergent vegetation, or any floating substitute such as planks of wood and fallen branches, into which it can oviposit. Without question the Brown Hawker is one of the most tolerant of the British species in respect of water quality. It has been seen on several occasions by R.Gabb to oviposit through a film of surface oil seeping from a derelict vehicle in the Ashton canal.

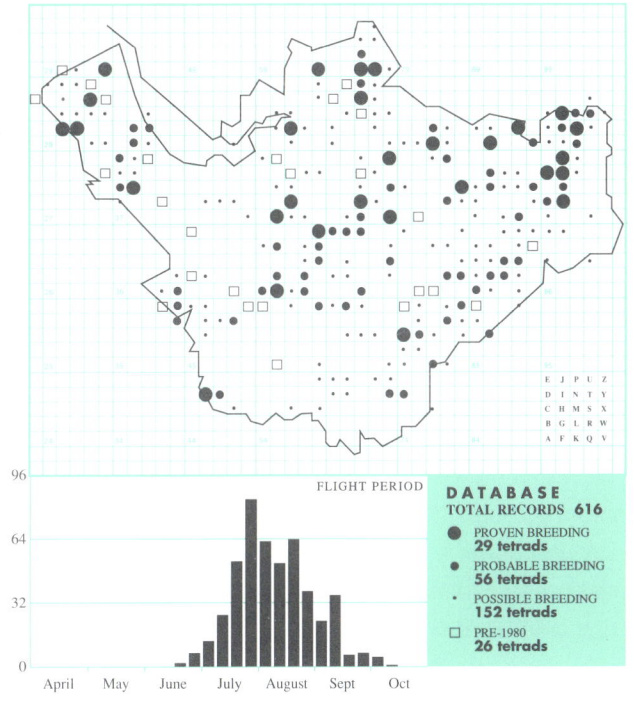

DATABASE
TOTAL RECORDS 616
● PROVEN BREEDING 29 tetrads
● PROBABLE BREEDING 56 tetrads
· POSSIBLE BREEDING 152 tetrads
□ PRE-1980 26 tetrads

The simplest description of its distribution in Cheshire is ubiquitous. It is undoubtedly the most likely species to be noticed by the casual observer. The Brown Hawker will be found on all suitable waters in unrecorded tetrads given sufficient recording effort. The earliest record to date is 23rd June 1986 by D.Kitching at Bollington (97D) and the latest record is 6th October 1985 by G.Cleland near the River Weaver (57T).

EMPEROR DRAGONFLY
Anax imperator
Leach, 1815

FIELD NOTES

The Emperor, Britain's largest dragonfly, seems to patrol ceaselessly in good weather from early in the day until dusk. It flies relatively high above the water and is prone to making sudden vertical dashes. The first confirmed sighting in Cheshire showed this behaviour with the insect on one occasion flying up to an estimated one hundred feet to make contact with a second dragonfly. The two tumbled down locked in combat with the second insect turning out to be another male Emperor, much to the surprise of the observer, J.Smith. For a period both males occupied territories on adjacent ponds with occasional boundary disputes. Any other species of dragonfly approaching the water was immediately repelled.

CHESHIRE STATUS AND DISTRIBUTION

In its main breeding range further south in the country this species is most commonly found in ponds and lakes having a good shelter belt with a substantial fringe of emergent vegetation. It is known to breed in a variety of habitats including marginally brackish waters and at newly created sites. Sightings in Cheshire have been made at large lakes and at a series of relatively small field ponds.

The nearest breeding colony to Cheshire at Ainsdale National Nature Reserve in Lancashire has declined substantially over the past few years. Within Cheshire a single historic record has been traced from Oakmere (56T), made by Cynthia Longfield on 30th July 1955.

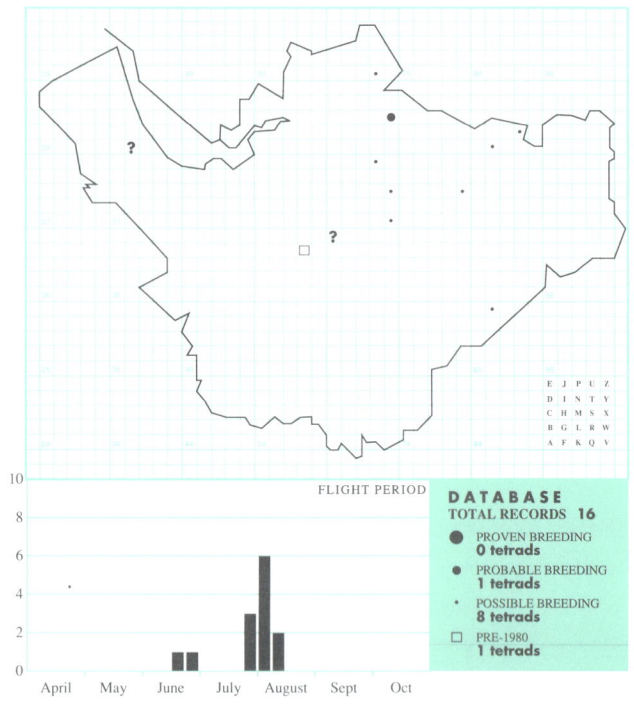

DATABASE
TOTAL RECORDS 16
- PROVEN BREEDING 0 tetrads
- PROBABLE BREEDING 1 tetrads
- POSSIBLE BREEDING 8 tetrads
- PRE-1980 1 tetrads

During the period of the present recording scheme two uncorroborated sightings were made by observers who were very familiar with the species. These were at Winsford (66M/S) in 1983 and from Gull Pool (66E) on 28th June 1986 by L.Thickett. Until 1990 the only confirmed record was made by J.Smith on 22nd June 1989. Two males were observed at a group of field ponds near Handforth (88R) just on the Greater Manchester boundary. One of these certainly stayed for two weeks.

It appeared that the Emperor Dragonfly was just a vagrant to Cheshire, then, in the splendid summer of 1990 no fewer than eight individual specimens were found at seven sites in Cheshire. The highlight was a pair, with the female observed ovipositing, on two ponds at High Legh near Knutsford (68X). These ponds will be carefully monitored for emergence/exuviae over the next few years. Undoubtedly this number of observations over a relatively limited area of Cheshire completely underestimates the true numbers of this species to have arrived in the county during 1990. This species was recorded at Lindow Common (88F) in both 1990 and 1991.

ritories. On return to the water they invariably patrol very low down at the base of the reeds, flying in between and clattering their wings against the stems as they feed and search for females. This sound can be a good pointer to their presence. In these respects their behaviour is similar to the Common Hawker (*Aeshna juncea*). The female is much more secretive and is more rarely seen except during the immediate post-emergence period. Mating frequently takes place in nearby trees with the female returning to the water to lay eggs into plant stems and floating vegetation.

CHESHIRE STATUS AND DISTRIBUTION

This species has declined nationally due to the destruction of fenland drainage channels and ditches which form its favoured breeding habitat. It also breeds on lakes and slow moving rivers. The presence of reedbeds is one feature which seems to be common to many of these sites. Other factors which determine the choice of breeding site are not fully known as apparently ideal and identical waters close to proven breeding areas in Cheshire are not colonised.

HAIRY DRAGONFLY
Brachytron pratense
(Müller, 1764)

FIELD NOTES

The Hairy Dragonfly is the earliest of the Anisoptera to emerge. It is rarely seen flying except in bright sunshine and quickly disappears if the weather becomes cloudy. It is also strongly territorial, males frequently clashing with other males and with other species such as the Four-spotted Chaser (*Libellula quadrimaculata*). As with all Anisoptera it can be found away from water during the maturation period. Males are also prone to make excursions on circuits away from the water after having established their ter-

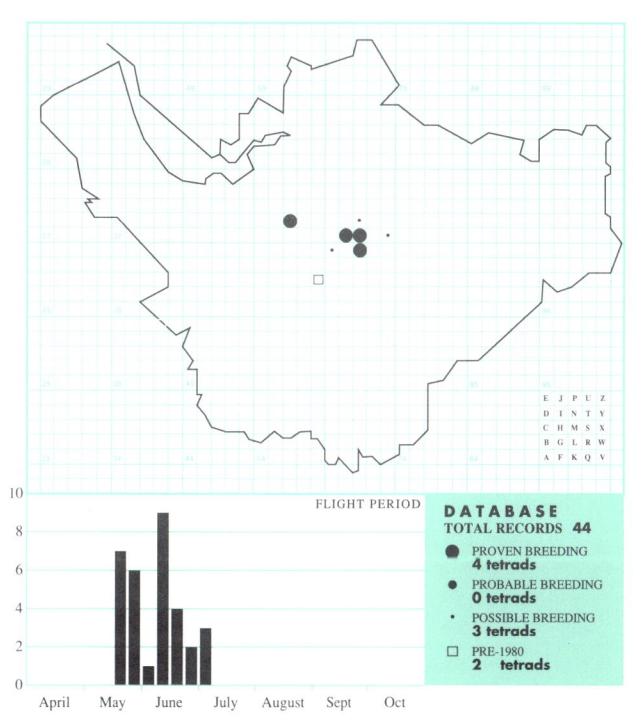

DATABASE
TOTAL RECORDS 44
● PROVEN BREEDING
  4 tetrads
● PROBABLE BREEDING
  0 tetrads
· POSSIBLE BREEDING
  3 tetrads
□ PRE-1980
  2 tetrads

On 2nd June 1985 a large-bodied dragonfly flew along the edge of the reedbed at the north-western corner of Hatchmere (57L). B.Bailey and R.Gabb realised the significance in recognising this as a male Hairy Dragonfly. It was the first confirmed sighting in Cheshire for nearly 25 years! Coincidentally, on the same day and at the same site, B.Walker independently recorded this species. Returning a fortnight later he saw two males and a female which was laying eggs. Previous historic records had come from Oulton Park (56X) in 1961 (D.Burn), Newchurch Common (66E) in 1945 (C.Longfield) and Hatchmere (57L) in 1943 (H.Burrows). A forecast in the 1985 Cheshire County Report for this species to be discovered at other sites proved correct. Gull Pool (66E) was the next site found by L.Thickett in 1986. D.Kitching made a major find in 1988 on the by-passed stretch of the River Weaver where it slowly meanders along the Vale Royal lock cut (66R-67F/K). He counted no fewer than 14 individuals in 67F on 28th May 1989. The most recent new site to be found is at Billinge Green (67N) in 1989. This is a brine subsidence flash adjacent to the Trent and Mersey Canal. Breeding has been confirmed in four tetrads with possible breeding in a further three. The Hairy Dragonfly is a most important species to Cheshire in respect of its declining national status.

The earliest record to date is 20th May 1989 by D.Jeffers on the River Weaver at Vale Royal (67K). The latest record is 4th July 1991 by D.Kitching at Vale Royal (66P/67K).

CLUB-TAILED DRAGONFLY
Gomphus vulgatissimus
(Linnaeus, 1758)

FIELD NOTES

This species is confined to rivers in Britain with the highest numbers being found on the Severn, Thames, Wye and their tributaries. They seem to prefer to emerge from the shallower and more slowly moving stretches of the river. These stretches often coincide with the flatter, trampled areas of the river bank and exuviae can sometimes be found lying in the footprints where cattle have come down to drink. The Club-tailed Dragonfly is not a "fast mover". It tends to fly rather slowly and it frequently rests for long periods on stones or on bankside vegetation. Until reaching maturity it may be encountered in woodland rides which can be quite a long distance from the river. During mating the pair often fly up into trees with the female returning alone to the river to lay eggs.

CHESHIRE STATUS AND DISTRIBUTION

The upper reaches of the Rivers Severn and Dee flow relatively close to each other and some time ago a hypothesis was put forward for the movement of this species from the Severn to the Dee. The discovery of an exuviae on the River Dee in Cheshire on 8th June 1985 by P.Adams, R.Merritt and R.Gabb must rank as one of the most significant and exciting British records in recent years. It was found one mile northwest of Farndon (35X) and was by far the most northerly record in Britain. Almost a year later to the day the first Cheshire adult was found by R.Gabb and S.Holland 5 kilometres further upstream at Caldecott (45F) on June 7th 1986.

The Club-tailed Dragonfly is one of two species to be found in Cheshire since 1985 which had never previously been recorded in the county. Only 8 records of exuviae and 5 records of adults have been received since these dates. The River Dee flows through 11 tetrads in Cheshire, from Shocklach down to Chester. Proof of breeding has been achieved in 6 of these tetrads through exuviae having been found on the banks. Possible breeding has been recorded by the observation of an adult in one other tetrad. No females have been seen ovipositing on the river. Clearly this species is even more sparsely distributed on the Dee compared with other British rivers where it is also a scarce dragonfly. All records have been made during a three week period between May 24th and June 14th each year. Searches between the above dates in tetrads 45D/E and 46B/C over future years will almost certainly complete the Cheshire picture. The River Gowy flows within 5 kilometres of the Dee and could possibly provide further suitable breeding habitat for the Club-tailed Dragonfly in Cheshire.

DOWNY EMERALD
Cordulia aenea
(Linnaeus, 1758)

FIELD NOTES

This is the only "Emerald" dragonfly to be found in Cheshire. In Britain it may be found in acidic, neutral and occasionally alkaline waters. There is a preference for sheltered sites with substantial surrounding woodland. Over the period of the recording scheme first sightings of the Downy Emerald have most frequently been made as it flies rapidly along woodland rides at treetop height during the maturation period. Mating has only been observed near to water with the females subsequently ovipositing alone. Males tend to spend long periods on territorial patrol.

CHESHIRE STATUS AND DISTRIBUTION

Almost certainly this dragonfly has the distinction of being Cheshire's scarcest breeding species. It is probably confined to one cluster of acidic pools surrounded by Forestry Commission woodland and breeding has only been proven at Gull Pool (56Z/66E). The maximum number of adults ever seen was 10 individuals recorded by L.Hall on 20th June 1989. Numbers seem to be increasing.

The Downy Emerald has a short flight period and is most commonly seen during June. The earliest sighting on record is 27th May 1988 by B.Shaw at Abbots Moss (56Z) and the latest is by D.Kitching at Gull Pool (56Z) on 22nd July 1987. Ovipositing was also observed on this relatively late date. This corresponds almost exactly with the flight period for the rest of Britain. Cheshire is fortunate in being one of the few counties with a breeding population away from the south of England.

Some of the most interesting records are those from pre-1980. The Downy Emerald was recorded at Petty Pool (66J/67A) by Brooke in 1882 (Lancashire & Cheshire Fauna Committee record). This constitutes one of the oldest records we have found. H.L.Burrows also recorded this species at Wybunbury Moss (65V) in 1956, further underlining the past importance of this site before it was severely damaged by pollution. The other early records all relate to Abbots Moss (56Z). There was also a possible sighting of two males at Little Budworth Common on 11th June 1990 by D. Wright. Whilst there was no corroboration of this record it is always likely that adults dispersing from Gull Pool will be found prospecting suitable habitat such as this.

KEELED SKIMMER
Orthetrum coerulescens
(Fabricius, 1798)

FIELD NOTES

The Keeled Skimmer is most likely to be found near sphagnum pools or wet heathland. Its fast flight at low level leads to the name Skimmer. It does require some open water and elsewhere in the country it has been found breeding in seepages of slow flowing deep water.

This species regularly patrols across wet boggy areas, stopping frequently at favoured perches or on the ground. The male flies low and erratically, often at the edges of open water. It is a wary dragonfly but can be approached particularly when ageing. The Keeled Skimmer is not strongly territorial and several may be found together without obvious conflict. Neither is the species very aggressive although, like most dragonflies, it will fly up to investigate intruders. One useful identification feature is the habit of settling with the wings held forward and pointing down similar to the posture adopted by Darters (*Sympetrum* spp.).

CHESHIRE STATUS AND DISTRIBUTION

This is the only Skimmer to have been confirmed in Cheshire and it must be regarded as an occasional visitor. The sole record in Cheshire during the period since 1980 was at Risley Moss by C.Young on 1st August 1984. Two of the earlier historic records were also made in similar habitat, both at Oakmere (56T), by J.Arkle in August 1892 and C.Longfield on 30th July 1955, but some sixty years apart. The third historic record is for Bidston (29V) on the Wirral in 1900.

The species is clearly a vagrant to the county. It should be looked for in good summers on any of the mosses during July and August.

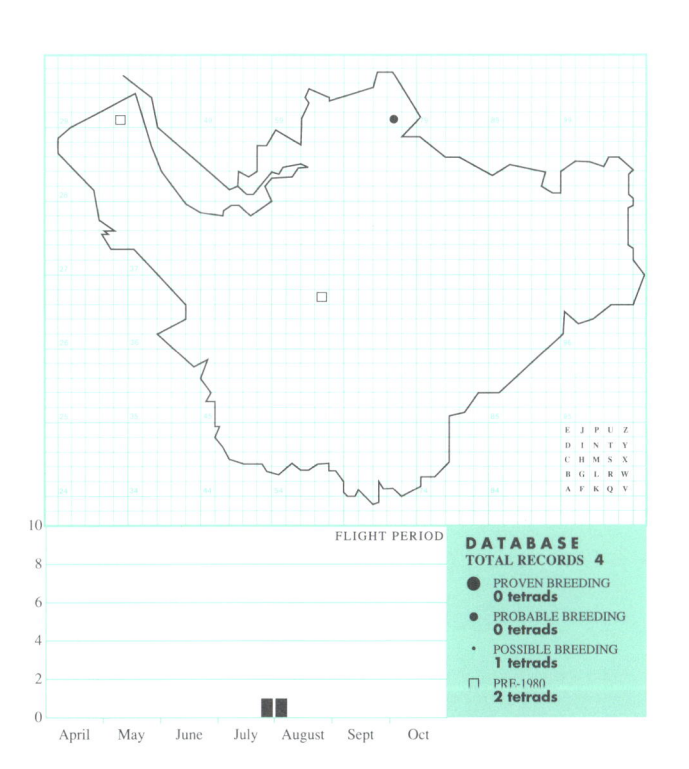

BROAD-BODIED CHASER
Libellula depressa
Linnaeus, 1758

FIELD NOTES

Aggressive, territorial, migratory, and approachable are all adjectives which spring to mind in describing this dragonfly. The male vigorously defends a well established territory in a similar manner to the Four-spotted Chaser (*Libellula quadrimaculata*). Areas of shallow water with gently shelving sides and with little or no vegetation appear to be ideal for breeding. Water chemistry does not seem to be critical as this species is known to breed in both eutrophic field ponds and in acidic heathland waters. Several years of observations have shown that dispersal takes place en masse some three weeks after emergence.

Middlewood Way (97I/J), the most carefully studied site, had many dragonflies on one day and on the next the majority had gone. Records were received from surrounding sites immediately afterwards. Both males and older females have been observed making circular patrols over water. This contrasts with the Four-spotted Chaser which tends to make brief, straight line forays. Ovipositing always seems to take place by abdomen dipping over shallow water at the muddy edge of the pond or ditch rather than into deeper water.

CHESHIRE STATUS AND DISTRIBUTION

The Broad-bodied Chaser is not common in Cheshire. It shows a marked preference for newly created waters which are well sheltered and is only recorded breeding on a few scattered sites. Its sudden appearance at newly established ponds underlines its migratory tendencies and post-breeding adults have often been seen at apparently unsuitable waters some distance from the known established sites. The main Middlewood Way breeding site has been studied in detail by D.Kitching. This pond and ditch system, specifically designed and managed in a disused railway cutting, was systematically cleared in sections between 1983 and 1988 in an attempt to create new habitat. Numbers rose from an initial record of 4 insects in 1983 to a peak emergence of 134 in 1986. They then declined until none was found in 1989. This occurred despite considerable effort by the Cheshire Countryside Management Service to maintain ideal breeding conditions. This reduction may also have been due in part to the introduction of Sticklebacks by well-meaning visitors.

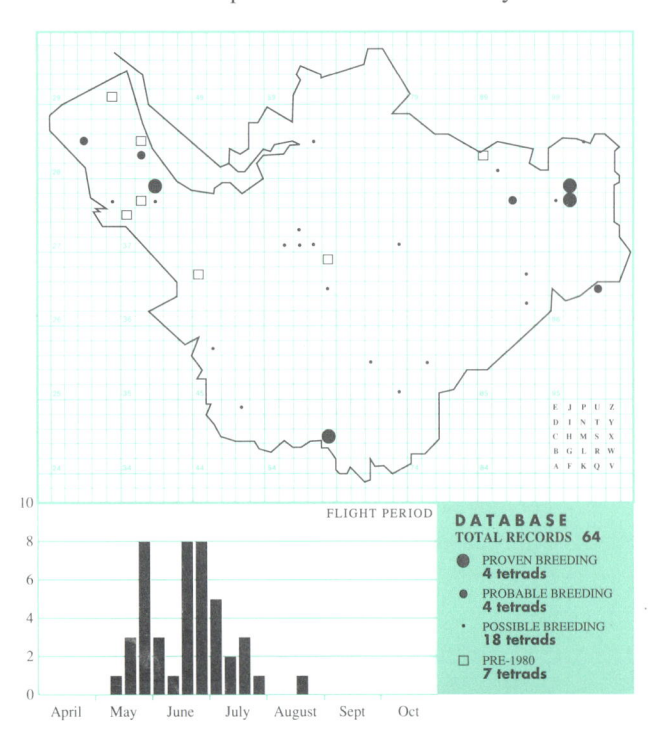

The other breeding site was at Bebington (37P) on the Wirral which is almost as far west as possible from the Middlewood Way. The Broad-bodied Chaser has also been observed ovipositing at three other sites; Royden Park (28M), again on the Wirral, Alderley Edge (87N) and in a trout farm at Wincle (96S) which is well into the Pennine edge. Sites in the other 15 tetrads where the species has been seen are scattered throughout the county, which confirms the tendency for this species to prospect over long distances. Further survey work will undoubtedly prove breeding in south-west Cheshire.

The earliest date this species has been recorded in the county is 10th May 1987 by D.Kitching at Middlewood Way (97I/J) and the latest date on 25th August 1985 was also by D.Kitching at the same site. This shows the very long flight period of the Broad-bodied Chaser. Peak emergence in all but one year at the Middlewood Way was during the second week of June. In 1987 it was three weeks earlier due to an unusually warm spell.

FOUR-SPOTTED CHASER
Libellula quadrimaculata
Linnaeus, 1758

FIELD NOTES

Breeding is confined to still, lowland waters across the Plain in all the suitable acidic habitats. The male Four-spotted Chaser is similar to the Broad-bodied Chaser (*Libellula depressa*) in being very territorial. Having established a territory on a stretch of water it patrols backwards and forwards pausing for occasional short rests on a selected perch. This flight pattern differs in being linear and parallel to the bank in comparison with the more circuitous route often taken by the Broad-bodied Chaser. It is much less approachable. The males are particularly aggressive, making very fast dashes to encounter other males encroaching upon their territory. The Four-spotted Chaser will also attack other large species such as the Emperor Dragonfly (*Anax imperator*). This was observed during the 1989 sighting of the Emperor Dragonfly in Cheshire. Females are seldom seen other than when mating or ovipositing. Egg laying is carried out by dipping the abdomen into the water, usually well away from the edge. Attention is often first drawn to the Four-spotted Chaser by the aerial clashing of wings whilst fighting or during the brief mating period. Sightings can be expected almost anywhere as this species is well known for its migratory behaviour.

CHESHIRE STATUS AND DISTRIBUTION

This species is most typically found in lakes and ponds which have abundant marginal vegetation. It is most numerous in acidic waters including bog pools and it can even be found in brackish water sites near the coast .

Looking at the Cheshire distribution map the main breeding populations correlate exactly with the principal acid bogs and associated heathland. Moving from east to west across the county these sites are Danes Moss (97A), Lindow Moss (88F), Lower Moss Wood (77X), Risley Moss (69Q), Gull Pool (56Z/66E), Little Budworth (56X), Oakmere (56P) and Black Lake (57F). Where the Four-spotted Chaser has been found breeding away from these sites it seems to be in smaller ponds and such colonisation has only been temporary. Examples are at a private pond in Bollington (97D) and a garden pond in Oldcastle Parish (44M). Other records are generally of single adults at widely scattered ponds. Even on smaller waters the numbers of this species to emerge and of males on territory can be quite considerable. For example 29 males were counted with territories around the lake at Lindow Common (88F) in June 1989.

The earliest record to date is 30th April 1990 at Little Budworth Common (56X) by D.Wright and the latest record is 19th August 1984 at Delamere Station (57K) by S.Hind.

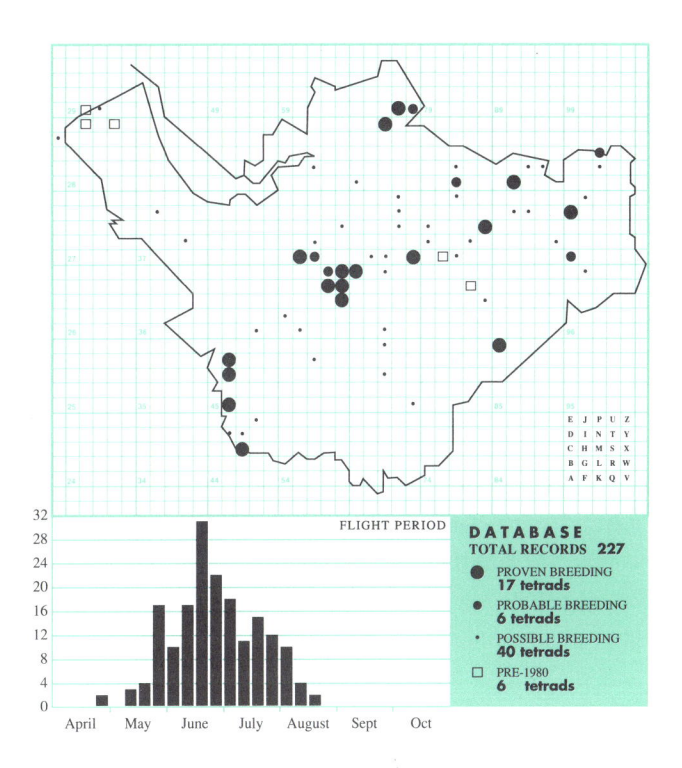

DATABASE
TOTAL RECORDS 227
● PROVEN BREEDING 17 tetrads
● PROBABLE BREEDING 6 tetrads
· POSSIBLE BREEDING 40 tetrads
□ PRE-1980 6 tetrads

WHITE-FACED DARTER
Leucorrhinia dubia
(Vander Linden, 1825)

FIELD NOTES

The White-faced Darter is a species which has exacting habitat requirements to enable it to breed satisfactorily. The type of habitat where it is found in numbers is similar throughout Britain. Its principal requirements are shallow peaty pools with a considerable amount of healthy sphagnum cover. Blanket bog, and in Cheshire the classic schwingmoor, with areas of nearby heathland, heather and small trees for shelter are also clearly favoured. This type of habitat has rapidly declined in the county. It is still changing with the encroachment of birch scrub into the sphagnum and with a general lowering of the water table but Cheshire still has some of the most important sites in England for this species.

The White-faced Darter is often abundant at favoured sites, but can be an inconspicuous dragonfly away from the water. It is easily disturbed whilst the observer is some distance from where it has settled and may often first be seen flying fast and low into further clumps of heather. Although territorial it doesn't seem particularly aggressive. Pairing can last for quite a long time but the female lays eggs into water or wet sphagnum unaccompanied by the male.

CHESHIRE STATUS AND DISTRIBUTION

The White-faced Darter is the most important Cheshire species with regard to its national status. It has been abundant in the Delamere area over the post 1980 period. This was so in 1989 when over thirty exuviae were collected in a 2 square metre area of *Juncus* species at the edge of Gull Pool (56Z/66E). Lesser numbers also breed at Black Lake (57F), a Cheshire Conservation Trust Reserve, some 6 kilometres away. These are the only known breeding sites but they must rank very highly in England. Certainly the numbers to be found in Surrey and Shropshire are less significant, which makes Cheshire one of the most southerly strongholds for the species in Britain. Walking along the rides through the woods near Shemmy Moss (56Z) in late May will provide excellent views.

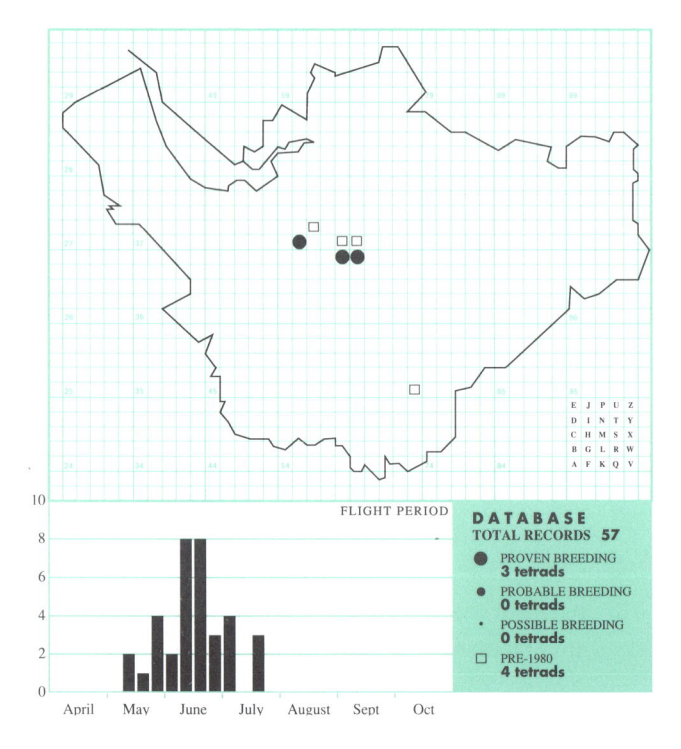

DATABASE
TOTAL RECORDS 57
● PROVEN BREEDING
  3 tetrads
● PROBABLE BREEDING
  0 tetrads
· POSSIBLE BREEDING
  0 tetrads
□ PRE-1980
  4 tetrads

There is no evidence of migration and the White-faced Darter remains within a short distance of its breeding site. This can be confirmed in Cheshire

Hatchmere

Hairy Dragonfly (*Brachytron pratense*)

Shemmy Moss

White-faced Darter (*Leucorrhinia dubia*)

Churton Marl Pit

Variable Damselfly (*Coenagrion pulchellum*)

River Dee at Farndon

Club-tailed Dragonfly (*Gomphus vulgatissimus*)

where apparently ideal breeding habitat remains unoccupied only a few kilometres from the main colonies.

There are some very interesting pre-1980 records which clearly indicate a reduction in the number of breeding sites. The White-faced Darter was recorded from Petty Pool (67A/66E&J) in 1882 (Manchester Museum specimen), from Flaxmere(57L) by J.Dunlop in 1908 (Warrington Museum specimen), from Cuddington (57V) by C.R.Brown in May 1931 and most significantly from Wybunbury Moss (65V) by H.Burrows as recently as 1956 (*pers. comm. to A.W.Boyd*). Wybunbury Moss is very similar to Shemmy Moss (56Z) in being typical "schwingmoor". Superficially it still looks ideal habitat although the water underlying the sphagnum raft has suffered severe sewage pollution over the last few years. Seemingly this represents another lost breeding site which had probably supported a population since post-glacial times.

Observation in Cheshire shows that the flight period in the county is not typical of that generally noted in the literature. This suggests that late May is the normal early emergence period whereas the earliest record to date in Cheshire has been 10th May 1987 at Black Lake (57F) by B.Walker. The latest record is 16th July 1989 at Gull Pool (66E) by B.Smith and L.Hall.

BLACK DARTER
Sympetrum danae
(Sulzer, 1776)

FIELD NOTES

Displaying little pronounced territorial instinct and with individuals being found well away from their known breeding sites Britain's smallest dragonfly can nevertheless be abundant where it does breed with substantial numbers of both sexes, in varying degrees of maturity, congregating together. It is quite approachable and frequently sits in the sun although it can be restless at times, making short flights before settling into grasses. Males in particular can be seen over quite a wide area surrounding the best breeding sites. Breeding behaviour has been observed late in the season with copulation taking place during the first week in October. When the population reaches a peak during early August many have been seen caught in spiders' webs on the mosses.

CHESHIRE STATUS AND DISTRIBUTION

The Black Darter requires a quite specific habitat, namely acidic, boggy waters. It will breed in lakes, small ponds and ditches, often where there is some sphagnum cover although this is not essential. Numbers seem to be linked to the amount of adjacent

Yellow-winged Darter
Sympetrum flaveolum
(Linnaeus, 1758)

FIELD NOTES

The behaviour is again similar to other members of the Darter family but it is recorded as frequently settling lower down in the vegetation. It appears to fly less at breeding sites although it is clearly well able to migrate to Britain.

CHESHIRE STATUS AND DISTRIBUTION

This migrant species has been found most frequently in the south of England during recent years and it may well have bred near the coast. On the continent the Yellow-winged Darter is said to favour semi-acidic habitat and also water meadows and fish ponds. It appears to prefer smaller waters than the Red-veined Darter (*Sympetrum fonscolombei*), especially those with substantial edge vegetation. This species has been recorded only four times in Cheshire and all these records refer to the pre-

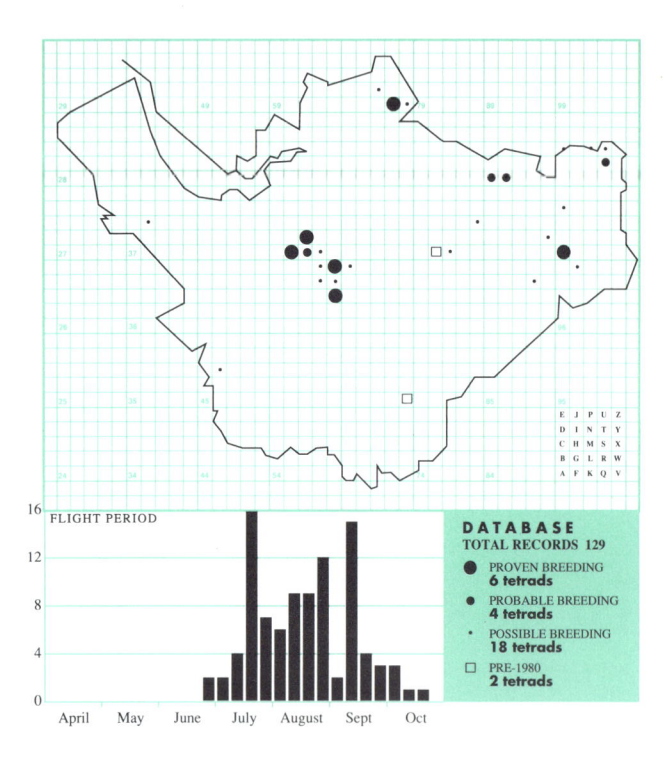

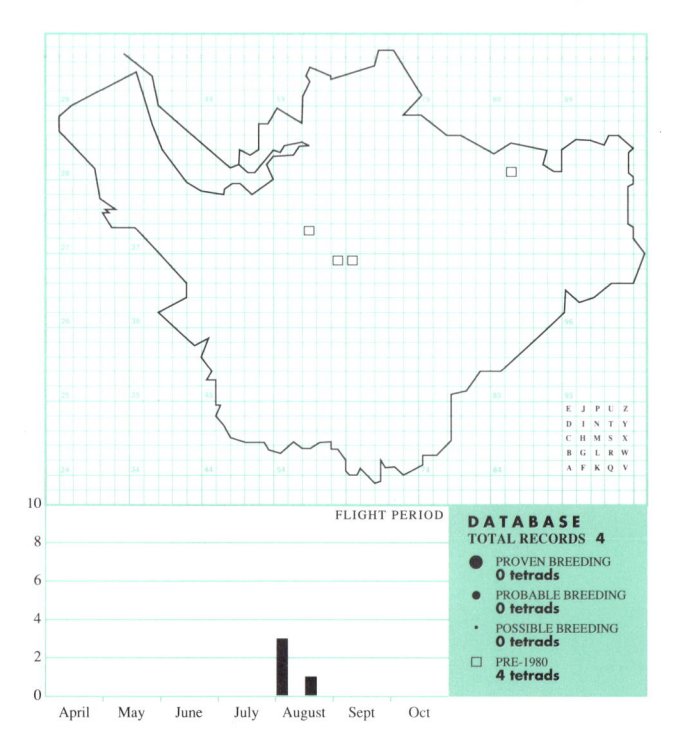

shelter and far more are found where there is substantial cover in comparison with open waters. In Cheshire this species occupies a similar niche to the Common Hawker (*Aeshna juncea*). The Black Darter ranges from the Pennine fringe and through the mosses of the Plain but it is much less of an upland insect than the Common Hawker.

It can be found at the following sites in Cheshire. From east to west across the County - Lyme Park (98R), Danes Moss (97A), Lindow Common (88F), Lower Moss Wood (77X), Risley Moss (69Q), Gull Pool (56Z/66E), Little Budworth (56X), Black Lake (57F) and Flaxmere (57L). Other casual records confirm the species' mobility. In favourable seasons there can be considerable populations at Danes Moss, Gull Pool and Risley. This is a fairly late species to emerge throughout the country.

The earliest Cheshire record to date is 25th June 1989 at Sandy Mere (56T) by S.Hind with the latest record being 19th October 1984 from Danes Moss (97A) by A.Savage.

1980 period. 1945 appears to have been a peak year for immigration with three of the records coming from that year. The records are from Flaxmere (57L) by J.Dunlop on 5th August 1907 (specimen in Warrington Museum), Abbots Moss (56Z) by H.Burrows on 4th August 1945 (Manchester Museum record and specimen), Newchurch Common (66E) by H.Britten on 2nd August 1945 (Manchester Museum record card) and Wilmslow Common (88F) by H.Burrows on 18th August 1945 (Manchester Museum record card).

RUDDY DARTER
Sympetrum sanguineum
(Müller, 1764)

FIELD NOTES

This dragonfly will be most noticeable during the warmest part of sunny days, sitting conspicuously on a favoured perch. From here it will fly out to catch insects or chase other dragonflies, frequently returning to the same spot. The females are less obvious and remain in the vegetation like the females of many other species. In Cheshire they were seen ovipositing by dropping eggs into wet mud and into the shallow water at the edges of ponds. The males were also seen resting on the dry, light coloured mud at the edges. The Ruddy Darter is approachable but perhaps less so than either the Common Darter (*Sympetrum striolatum*) or Black Darter (*Sympetrum danae*). It is undoubtedly migratory.

CHESHIRE STATUS AND DISTRIBUTION

The Ruddy Darter seems to prefer somewhat neglected waters and has not been seen at open, "tidy" ponds; field ponds which are well vegetated with rushes, horsetail, reedmace and bur-reed are ideal. If there are muddy margins so much the better.

It is the second of two species to have been discovered for the first time in Cheshire during the period of the present Tetrad Recording Scheme. Being superficially similar to the Common Darter (*Sympetrum striolatum*) this may account for it never having been recorded in Cheshire prior to 1985. The first record was made by B.Smith at a field pond on a private estate in 46G on 25th July 1985. Fortunately a clear colour photograph of one of the males showed conclusively that it was a Ruddy Darter and not the Common Darter. Searches at the same site during the following year provided no further records and it was thought at the time that the 1985 males may well have been casual visitors.

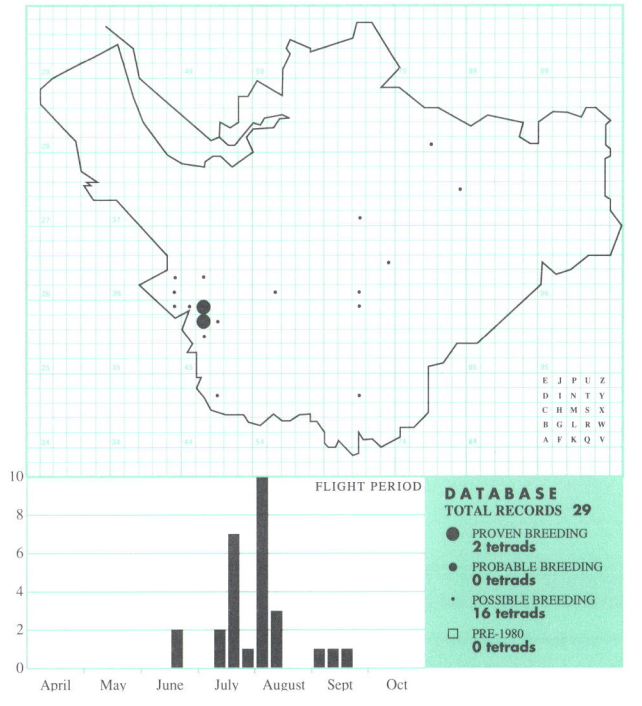

DATABASE
TOTAL RECORDS 29
● PROVEN BREEDING 2 tetrads
● PROBABLE BREEDING 0 tetrads
· POSSIBLE BREEDING 16 tetrads
□ PRE-1980 0 tetrads

However, photographs taken by L.Hall in 1986 and 1987 at Churton (45I/H) proved on closer examination to be of the Ruddy Darter. Since this time it has been found on a number of marl pits in the south-west of the county. The 19 records received to the end of 1990 have been spread over a relatively small area within the ten kilometre squares SJ35,36 and 44-46 which all contain large numbers of marl pits. During 1991, records were received for a number of new sites across Cheshire as far east as Tatton Park (78K) and Lower Moss Wood (77X), and future years will show whether this was due to an influx of migrants or reflects a change in the breeding range of this species. Breeding was proven in 1989. The earliest record to date is 22nd June 1990 at Churton (45I) by D.Kitching and the latest date is 20th September 1991 at Tatton Park (78K) by D.Jeffers.

RED-VEINED DARTER
Sympetrum fonscolombei
(Selys, 1840)

FIELD NOTES

Comments regarding the resident *Sympetrum* species apply equally to the Red-veined Darter which is also a strong flyer and is highly migratory. The reduction in available breeding habitat over the last few decades may have been lower on the continent than here but there is still less likelihood of occurrence than in pre-war years.

CHESHIRE STATUS AND DISTRIBUTION

The Red-veined Darter is one of two immigrant species found in Cheshire prior to the current recording scheme. On the continent the Red-veined Darter breeds in a wide range of habitats. In Britain it has been noticed most frequently at large pools which have extensive reed margins. As a migrant to this country it may be found anywhere there is suitable water.

Only two records have been discovered and both of these occurred prior to 1980. The first was from Oakmere (56J) by J.Arkle in 1892 (Lancashire & Cheshire Fauna Committee record) and the second was from Rostherne Mere (78L/M) by H.Burrows in July 1941, for which a voucher specimen exists in Manchester Museum.

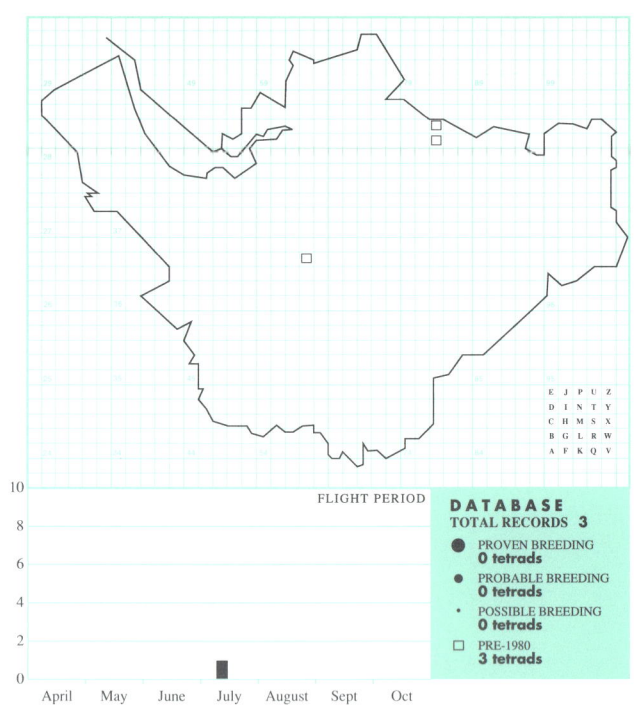

COMMON DARTER
Sympetrum striolatum
(Charpentier, 1840)

FIELD NOTES

The Common Darter is well known as a particularly inquisitive dragonfly. It is attracted to pale surfaces and will frequently land upon white clothing, which can be very frustrating for a photographer when it lands on their shirt! More usually it can be found sunning itself on bare soil, gravel paths and any lighter coloured ground surface. The male is aggressive and flies up from a favoured resting point to chase other males and larger dragonflies. Egg-laying takes place over water with the male and female generally flying in tandem. The female dips the tip of her abdomen into the water to disperse the eggs. This species is often the latest to be found on the wing, flying up to and even past the first frosts. Old specimens become very torpid on warm surfaces and can almost be picked up.

CHESHIRE STATUS AND DISTRIBUTION

In Britain there are few still water habitats where this species is unlikely to be found. It may also frequent canals and slow flowing rivers. Experience suggests that in Cheshire this species is found in greatest abundance on waters with open shallow margins. If the water is newly formed with adjacent light coloured stony areas or dry cattle-trampled mud so much the better. It can, however, be found elsewhere in lesser numbers where the habitat is more overgrown. It has not as yet been discovered on any moving water in the county and generally does not seem as widespread in its choice of breeding sites as comments in other literature might suggest. All breeding records to date have come from ponds and ditches.

The map shows a widespread distribution but the Common Darter does not live up to its name in being a common species in Cheshire. Its relative absence from the north-west and south-west of the county is difficult to explain. Bias in recording towards the east will partially account for this but the species would still be expected more frequently on the marl pits of the plain. The cluster of records from the Wirral and proof of breeding from a pool on Hilbre Island (18Y) are worthy of note. Other sites where some numbers have been observed are Little Budworth Common (56X), Woolston Eyes (68N/68P), Rixton Clay Pits (69V) and Danes Moss (97A).

The earliest record to date is 21st June 1988 from Runcorn Town Park (58L) and the latest record is 29th October 1988 from the Old Quay Canal (58G), both records being submitted by A.Parker.

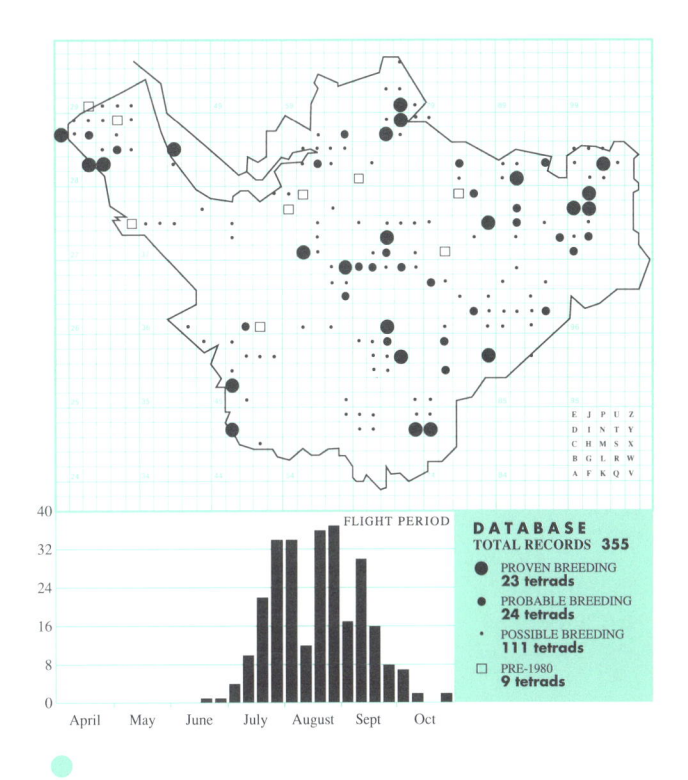

DATABASE
TOTAL RECORDS 355
● PROVEN BREEDING 23 tetrads
● PROBABLE BREEDING 24 tetrads
· POSSIBLE BREEDING 111 tetrads
□ PRE-1980 9 tetrads

'UNCORROBORATED' SPECIES RECORDS

Records of three other dragonflies (Anisoptera) have been submitted during the the present recording scheme. Regrettably none was confirmed by independent witness or photograph. All records, including those classified as historic (pre-1980), are listed below.

GOLDEN-RINGED DRAGONFLY
Cordulegaster boltonii
(Donovan, 1807)

This has been the most frequently recorded of the three species and there can be little doubt that casuals do appear in Cheshire. Records in the west of the county (SJ36/SJ46) may stem from vagrants originating in Clwyd. The record from SJ98 in the east was exciting as it came from a seemingly suitable site near a Pennine upland stream. But no further records have been made despite annual searches at likely breeding sites in the hills. The nearest breeding stream in the Derbyshire Pennines appears similar to those in Cheshire so it seems quite likely that this species will eventually be confirmed in the county. The uncorroborated records are as follows:

1890 Chester	46D	per Lancashire Recorder
1970 Hale	48R	R.Askew
August 1984 Nr Chester	36Y	B.Smith
11th August 1984 Lyme Park	98R	P.Garnett
6th August 1989 Mere	78F	S.Blamire

BLACK-TAILED SKIMMER
Orthetrum cancellatum
(Linnaeus, 1758)

The superb summer of 1989 provided an abundance of dragonfly records including sightings of a single male of this species at Lindow Common (88F) by P.Hughes and R.Doran, two Rangers from the Cheshire Countryside Management Service. Again, despite further searching by one of the authors, it was not re-located.

13th June 1989   88F   P.Hughes and R.Doran
Lindow Common

SCARCE CHASER
Libellula fulva
Müller, 1764

This is not a species one would expect in Cheshire. The superficial similarity of the male Scarce Chaser to the male Black-tailed Skimmer (Orthetrum cancellatum) might suggest that there had been a mis-identification. However, the accurate description submitted by M.Bailey the English Nature (formerly Nature Conservancy Council) Warden at the Rostherne Reserve makes this explanation improbable.

1st August 1989   78L   M.Bailey
Rostherne NNR

BANDED DEMOISELLE
Calopteryx splendens
(Harris, 1782)

FIELD NOTES

There is a courtship display similar to that found in the Beautiful Demoiselle (*Calopteryx virgo*) and care must be taken in differentiating between the females of the two Demoiselles. During sunny weather the Banded Demoiselle is a most conspicuous species.

Flights are made out in a loop over the river and back to the bank. Many specimens will congregate on vegetation growing in the river. As soon as the sun disappears the damselflies become surprisingly difficult to find deep down in the tall grasses and edge vegetation. Contrary to some descriptions this species can show a strong and quite fast direct flight, which will help expansion of its breeding sites if river water quality improves.

CHESHIRE STATUS AND DISTRIBUTION

The Banded Demoiselle is much the more likely of the two Demoiselle species to be seen in Cheshire. It prefers rather slower moving waters than the Beautiful Demoiselle. It also tolerates some silt and colouration but not any pollution. There is a preference for rivers with abundant edge vegetation and with the open sunny areas which are often found in meadows away from habitation. In Cheshire this species has a far more widespread and extensive distribution than the Beautiful Demoiselle, being found on long stretches of at least ten streams and rivers in habitat which mirrors the above description. Of specific interest however is the considerable number to be found on the relatively still waters in one of our canals and indeed wandering males are quite frequently seen along other canals or even flying across countryside without any breeding habitat nearby. This species is often found resting in vegetation at the edge of ponds near to the main rivers although there has been no evidence of breeding behaviour at still waters in Cheshire.

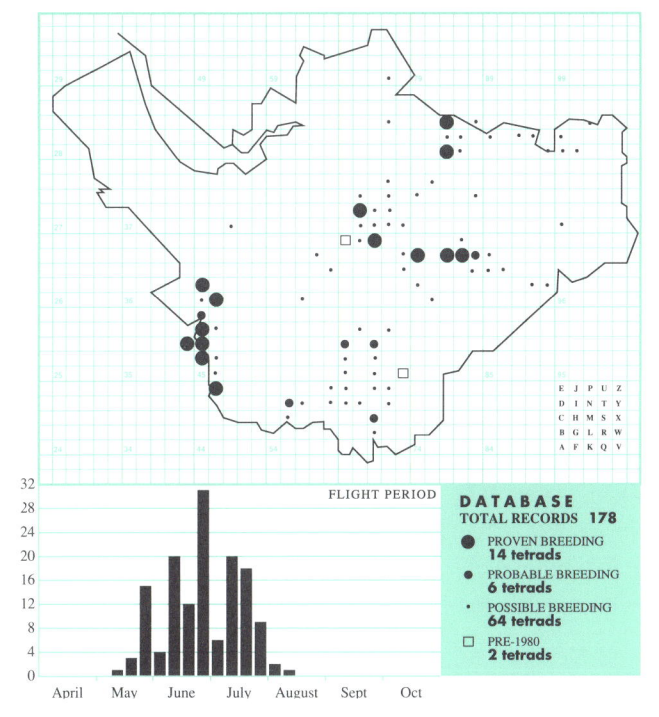

Placing a transparent overlay of the rivers and canals of Cheshire upon the distribution map would show the extent of this species along many of the county's waterways. The main rivers where it is found in abundance are the Dee from Shocklach (44J) to Eccleston (46B), the Weaver from Audlem (64L) to Northwich (67H), the Dane from near Congleton (86W) to Middlewich (76B), the Dean from Woodford (98A) to Lacey Green (88L) and the Birkin Brook/Tatton Mere Stream (78L/M). Considerable numbers have been reported from the slow moving Llangollen Canal between 54H and 65C.

The flight period is long. In Cheshire it has ranged from an earliest date of 13th May 1990 by K.Darwin on the River Dean (88V) to a latest date of 10th August 1985 by B.Walker on the River Dee at Aldford (45D).

BEAUTIFUL DEMOISELLE
Calopteryx virgo
(Linnaeus, 1758)

DATABASE
TOTAL RECORDS 178
● PROVEN BREEDING 14 tetrads
● PROBABLE BREEDING 6 tetrads
• POSSIBLE BREEDING 64 tetrads
□ PRE-1980 2 tetrads

FIELD NOTES

The Beautiful Demoiselle is arguably the most striking of the British damselflies and it is one of a very few British species to have a discrete courtship ritual. Males will suddenly spread their wings showing metallic flashes, the actual display consisting of a semi-circular flight in front of females which culminates in a "dance" face first towards a potential partner. Females also wing-flash and raise their abdomens whilst ovipositing to deter intruding males. They oviposit into plant stems and will totally submerge with their partners providing protection from other males. Non-breeding males and females will congregate without aggression.

CHESHIRE STATUS AND DISTRIBUTION

Although both of the Demoiselle species occur in Cheshire the Beautiful Demoiselle has a much more restricted distribution. It is essentially a river species and only breeds in moving water. It seems to have a more restricted habitat than the Banded Demoiselle (*Calopteryx splendens*) preferring clean, clear streams which are fairly fast flowing over a stony, gravel or sandy base and which have extensive edge vegetation and tree cover. The Beautiful Demoiselle appears to be confined to the upper reaches of the River Weaver in Cheshire. The Banded Demoiselle is also recorded with it here, and elsewhere in Britain the two species do often share the same habitat.

It has been recorded between Audlem (64M) at the highest point and Reaseheath (65M) about 9 kilometres downstream. Numbers are quite low with the maximum count being 10 males and 5 females at Batherton Hall (64U) by A.Gradwell on 6th July 1987. Only 15 separate records have been submitted and therefore the extent of the distribution on the River Weaver remains unclear. No proof of breeding has been obtained but sightings have come from all but one year between 1980 and 1989. Three interesting casual records have been made well away from the river. The first was from Neston (27W) on the Wirral. In July 1986 B.Dickson identified a dead damselfly brought to him by school children from a local stream as being this species. The second sighting was made by R.Gabb, S.Hind and D.Kitching during a windy 20th June 1987 when one was seen to fly along a ride near Shemmy Moss (56Z). More recently P.Griffiths, R.Robinson and P.Atherton recorded males on 18th June 1989 somewhat nearer to the River Weaver at Wybunbury Brook (74E) and Wybunbury Moss (65V) near Nantwich.

Historic records have come mainly from the River Dee between Farndon (45C) and Eccleston (46B) although the absence of present day sightings suggests either a change in water quality or confusion with the Banded Demoiselle. One further unusual site was at Oulton Park Lake (56X) where a record was made on 23rd May 1959 (D.Burn).

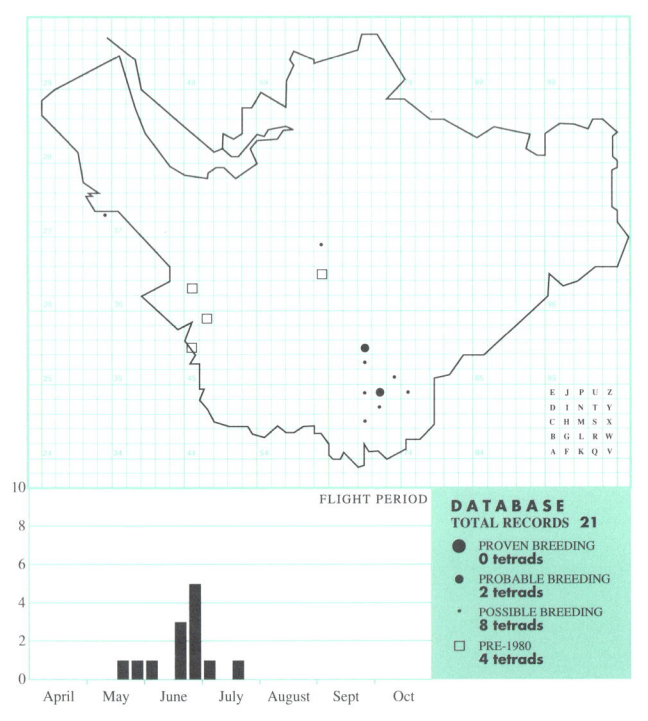

During the Tetrad Survey species have only been recorded between 18th June and 6th July, but this probably reflects the limited number of observations rather than the true flight period.

Emerald Damselfly
Lestes sponsa
(Hansemann, 1823)

FIELD NOTES

This is a sedentary species which flies infrequently and sits in the vegetation for long periods. Ovipositing into plant stems takes place with both the male and the female often descending below the surface of the water for long periods. This leads to reports of the male 'drowning' the female! Although the exuviae can be found quite readily, the adults are easily overlooked as their colouration blends so well with the background vegetation.

CHESHIRE STATUS AND DISTRIBUTION

This is the only Emerald Damselfly likely to be found in Cheshire as the Scarce Emerald (*Lestes dryas*) is confined to the east and south-east of England. The Emerald Damselfly is said to have a wide tolerance of breeding sites which range from acid to neutral or even brackish water, and from slow-moving to still waters including ditches. There is a requirement for shelter and in particular for extensive marginal vegetation which frequently consists of reeds and rushes.

In Cheshire this species seems to prefer acidic boggy areas, well vegetated lakes and marl pits.

There is a scattered distribution in Cheshire and it seems that the Emerald Damselfly has frequently been missed in the past. Very considerable numbers occur in north and east Cheshire at the acidic waters such as Danes Moss (97A), Lindow Moss (88F) and Risley Moss (69Q). Other acidic sites where the species is abundant are Melchett Mere (78K) and Gull Pool (56Z/66E). In the south-west it has been found in a substantial number of marl pits and will undoubtedly be discovered in many of those yet to be visited. On the Wirral there are sites at Thurstaston (28G) and it is one of the few species to have flown across the Dee estuary to Hilbre Island (18X) where it was recorded in 1987 by J.Daws.

This is a late species to emerge with the earliest record to date being 15th June 1988 at Sound Common (64E) by D.Kitching and the latest record being 30th September 1986 at Saltersley Moss (88F) by A.Gradwell.

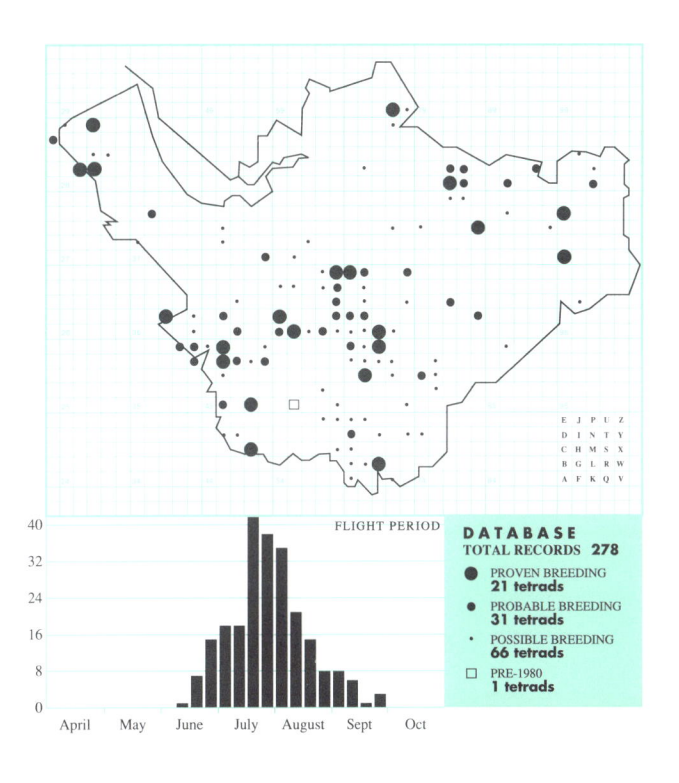

DATABASE
TOTAL RECORDS 278
- PROVEN BREEDING **21 tetrads**
- PROBABLE BREEDING **31 tetrads**
- POSSIBLE BREEDING **66 tetrads**
- PRE-1980 **1 tetrads**

Red-eyed Damselfly
Erythromma najas
(Hansemann, 1823)

FIELD NOTES

The Red-eyed Damselfly is a most attractive insect, although frequently it can only be seen at a distance as it sits on lily pads and pondweeds. Territory is established using a particular lily pad, piece of floating wood, or even a clump of algae, as a base. From here forays are made with the damselfly returning to the same point. Although it can appear quite aggressive it has been noticed by the authors that other species such as the Common Blue Damselfly (*Enallagma cyathigerum*) often 'win' the battles and displace the Red-eyed Damselfly. Ovipositing takes place into leaves and sometimes plant stems with the pair in tandem. Perhaps the most opportune time to obtain a close approach is during the maturation period when the species will sit in nearby hedges or edge vegetation.

CHESHIRE STATUS AND DISTRIBUTION

Other books list the most likely habitat as being larger ponds and lakes having abundant surface vegetation such as Water Lily pads and Pondweeds (*Potomageton* spp). Slow moving waters, including the meanders of quite large rivers, are also likely sites. In Cheshire it can be confirmed as a species which prefers larger waters with areas of emergent plants but this is by no means the exclusive habitat. Indeed, the Red-eyed Damselfly has been found on a number of quite small ponds and marl pits. Some of these ponds have little emergent vegetation although there is usually substantial edge vegetation. The species has been recorded at one site on the River Weaver where the water is slow moving with some plant cover.

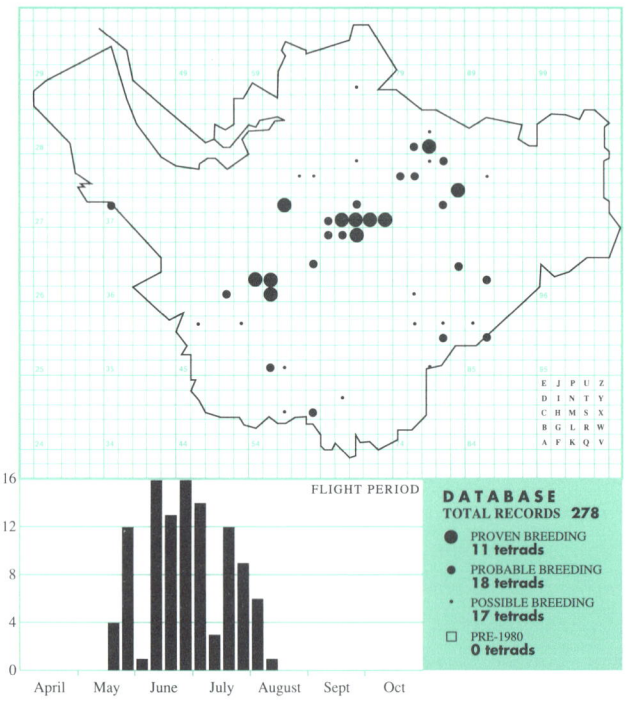

DATABASE
TOTAL RECORDS **278**
● PROVEN BREEDING **11 tetrads**
● PROBABLE BREEDING **18 tetrads**
· POSSIBLE BREEDING **17 tetrads**
□ PRE-1980 **0 tetrads**

The Red-eyed Damselfly is one species which has now been found in many more tetrads than would have been envisaged in 1980. The species has been confirmed at all the pre-1980 'historic' sites, namely Rode Pool (85D), Petty Pool (66E/67A), Cholmondeley (55F) and Hatchmere (57L). During the recent recording period a further 35 sites have been discovered. These range from an extremely small pool at Soss Moss (87I) to the stronghold covering several tetrads in Vale Royal mainly associated with the flashes such as Billinge Green (67V) and the River Weaver (66P/67F/K). Another group of records has come from marl pits at Tiverton (56F/G).

Scattered records throughout the rest of the county show no particular pattern but usually come from field ponds. In 1989 the first sighting of the Red-eyed Damselfly on the Wirral was made at Burton Mere Ponds (37B). Further survey work will surely reveal an even more extensive distribution.

The earliest record to date is 21st May 1989 from the River Weaver by P.Smith and R.Letsche. The latest record is 14th August 1982 at Hatchmere (57L) by S.Hind.

LARGE RED DAMSELFLY
Pyrrhosoma nymphula
(Sulzer, 1776)

FIELD NOTES

This species is one of the earliest to emerge in Cheshire. It is a sedentary damselfly flying mainly in the middle of the day. Ovipositing occurs with the pair in tandem. At some sites in the county numbers are very variable from year to year and it seems to be quite difficult to find the nymphs even where there are high numbers of adults.

CHESHIRE STATUS AND DISTRIBUTION

The Large Red Damselfly is described in the literature as occupying a catholic choice of breeding habitat. Apart from the usual field ponds it inhabits bogs, brackish water and slow moving rivers, particularly if these are unpolluted and have shelter with plenty of vegetation along the margins. In Cheshire it has been found in ponds, ditches, bogs, marshes and rivers so it might well be described as universal. There are gaps in the distribution however and it is by no means a common damselfly in some apparently suitable areas. It is also an upland species and can be found in ponds well into the Pennine edge, whilst on the Plain it is one of the few species which seem to be capable of tolerating ponds with almost total tree cover, providing there is a small patch of edge vegetation.

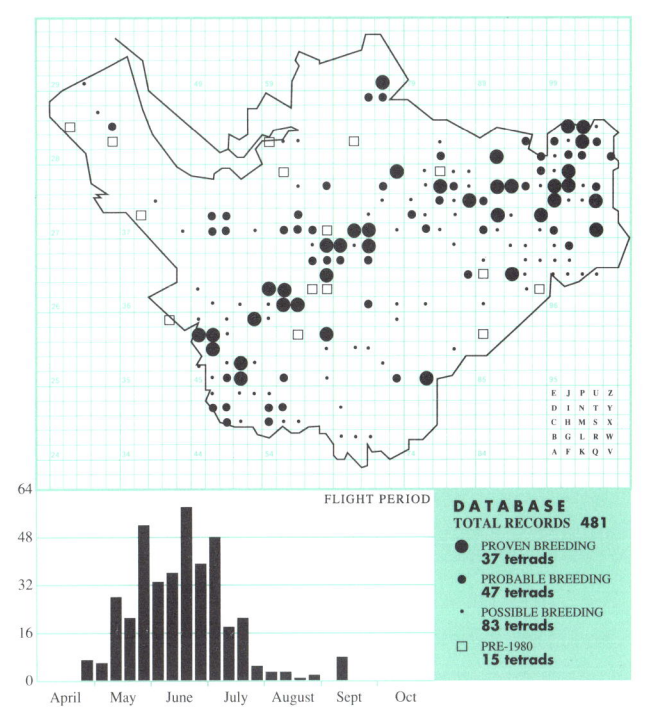

DATABASE
TOTAL RECORDS 481
PROVEN BREEDING 37 tetrads
PROBABLE BREEDING 47 tetrads
POSSIBLE BREEDING 83 tetrads
PRE-1980 15 tetrads

It appears to be found more frequently in the east although this may well be due to observational bias. At some sites, such as Danes Moss (97A), numbers can be considerable but more often at field ponds there are just a few pairs. In marked contrast to the surprisingly few records from the Wirral, large populations occur on the River Weaver at Vale Royal (66P) and also on the Rivers Dee and Gowy.

The flight period is the longest of any Cheshire species with the earliest record being 24th April 1990 at Gull Pool (56Z/66E) by D.Kitching. The latest record to date is 10th September 1985 when a pair were observed ovipositing at Blakemere Moss (57K) by S.Hind.

BLUE-TAILED DAMSELFLY
Ischnura elegans
(Vander Linden, 1820)

FIELD NOTES

The female has a number of colour variations which can lead to initial identification difficulties. The species is often abundant however and these forms can all be recognised after a little practice.

This species is not particularly mobile, preferring to keep to the edge vegetation and seldom flying across open water. Males exhibit aggression and there are frequent threat displays with the wings being opened and the abdomen raised. Females oviposit alone into vegetation and may descend beneath the surface of the water where locally they have also been observed to move quite quickly across the bottom of shallow water.

CHESHIRE STATUS AND DISTRIBUTION

The abundance of the Blue-tailed Damselfly both in Cheshire and nationally suggests that it is able to breed successfully in a wide range of waters. It has been found in ponds, slow moving rivers, brackish coastal waters and it will even tolerate a degree of pollution. Neutral to alkaline sites are probably favoured although in Cheshire there are quite a number of acidic waters with large breeding populations. One necessary element in all habitats appears to be a measure of marginal vegetation.

The Blue-tailed Damselfly is the most widespread of all the Cheshire species. Indeed it is likely to be found wherever there is any suitable water and it is often the only species at the most marginally suitable sites. This damselfly has one of the longest flight perods and the earliest record is 10th May 1987 at Antrobus (68F) by R.Gabb whilst the latest date is 12th September 1985 at Pursefield Pool (98K) by S.Hind.

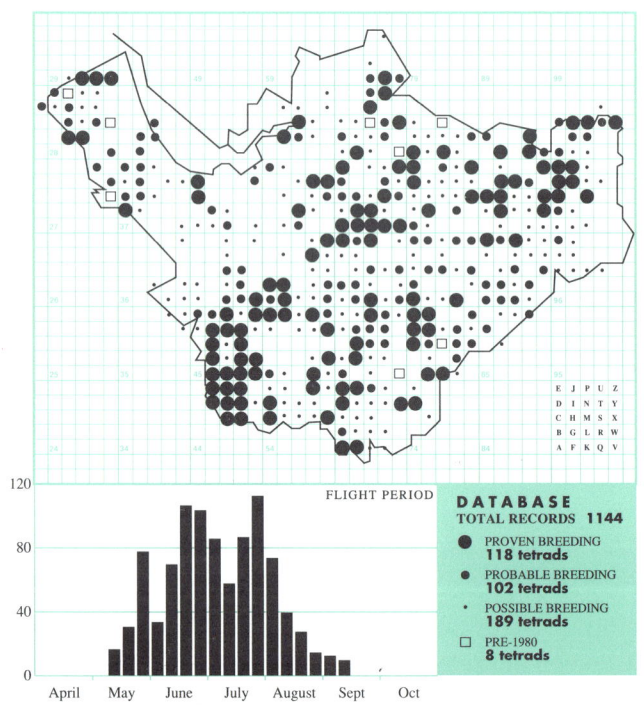

DATABASE
TOTAL RECORDS 1144
- PROVEN BREEDING 118 tetrads
- PROBABLE BREEDING 102 tetrads
- POSSIBLE BREEDING 189 tetrads
- PRE-1980 8 tetrads

COMMON BLUE DAMSELFLY
Enallagma cyathigerum
(Charpentier, 1840)

FIELD NOTES

The Common Blue Damselfly can often be seen flying strongly in considerable numbers across open water. Indeed it frequently flies on quite windy days with individuals all heading into the prevailing wind, or even backwards if it is particularly strong! Males can be quite aggressive. Amongst the damselflies it is one species which can be found some distance from the likely emergence water. One other interesting observation is that when landing on edge vegetation it perches horizontally with the abdomen held almost at right angles to the stem.

CHESHIRE STATUS AND DISTRIBUTION

This is another species which occupies most types of habitat. In the literature it is said to be found in ponds, lakes, peat bogs, stagnant pools, brackish waters and, more rarely, slow flowing streams. Large open waters with ample marginal vegetation is the preferred habitat which is frequently quoted. In Cheshire the Common Blue certainly lives up to its name in being common at many of the more acidic waters.

In addition to several riverine sites in the county it has also been found in a high proportion of tetrads on much smaller waters such as marl pits.

Our knowledge of the status of this species has improved quite significantly. It is clearly much more widely distributed and more abundant than was thought during the early years of the present recording scheme. In the west of the county there are only a scattering of records for the Wirral but it is another of the few species to have been found on Hilbre Island. Central and eastern Cheshire show numerous records, and similar to the Large Red Damselfly (*Pyrrhosoma nymphula*), it is a species to be found well into the Pennine edge. Proof of breeding has been obtained in one of the most easterly tetrads at a millpond in Wildboarclough (96Z). Other eastern sites are the mill lodge at Lumbhole Mill (98V) and at Waterside Paper Mill, Disley (98X). The species is extremely abundant at the mossland sites, in particular at Gull Pool (56Z/66E) and Risley Moss (69Q). A central river site is on the Weaver at Aston (57N). In the south and south-west low numbers can be found on many of the smaller marl pits with higher numbers on the larger waters such as at Baddiley Mere (54Z). Records have also come from the River Dee at Aldford (45E) and the River Gowy at Bridge Trafford (47K).

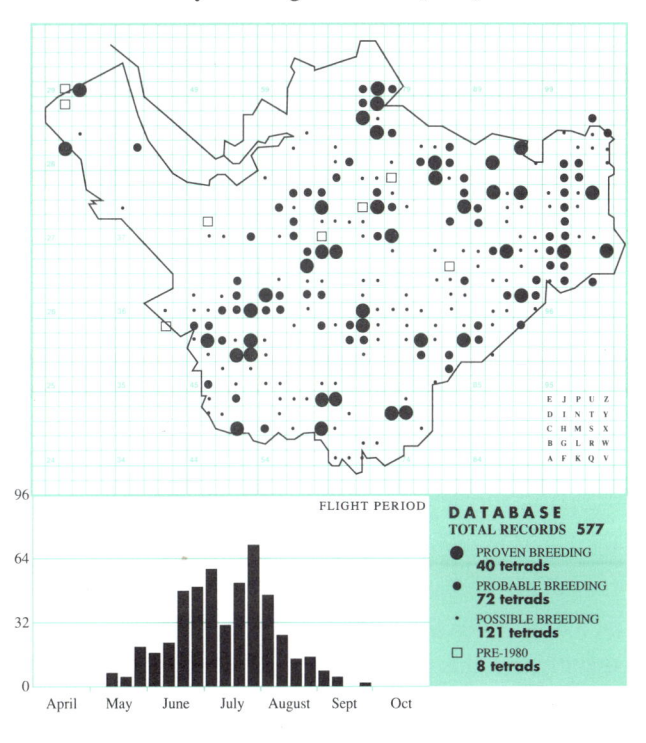

FLIGHT PERIOD

DATABASE
TOTAL RECORDS 577
- ● PROVEN BREEDING **40 tetrads**
- ● PROBABLE BREEDING **72 tetrads**
- · POSSIBLE BREEDING **121 tetrads**
- □ PRE-1980 **8 tetrads**

The Common Blue Damselfly has a long flight period. The earliest record is 10th May 1989 by D.Kitching at Lindow Common (88F) and the latest record to date is 29th September 1985 made by R.Gabb and S.Hind at Taxmere (76R).

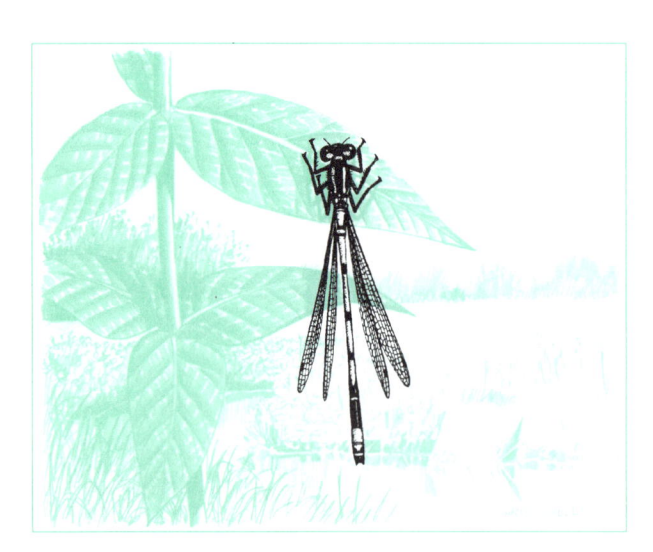

AZURE DAMSELFLY
Coenagrion puella
(Linnaeus, 1758)

FIELD NOTES

In a similar manner to some of the other 'blue' damselflies, the Azure Damselfly is low flying and frequently settles in the vegetation for long periods. It seems to congregate in large numbers particularly when the weather is poor.

CHESHIRE STATUS AND DISTRIBUTION

This is another damselfly species which is able to breed in a wide variety of habitat. Ditches, ponds, canals and slow moving rivers are occupied provided they include plenty of vegetation. All these types of habitat are used in Cheshire which also includes bogs as a further breeding site. It has been found quite frequently in fields and along hedgerows well away from water. During windy weather considerable numbers can be seen on the lee side of sheltering hedges. Despite the undoubted preference for well vegetated sites it is a species which can be found in ponds with little vegetation. At such ponds it is usually the only species to be found.

The Azure Damselfly has therefore a wide distribution and is probably the second commonest damselfly in Cheshire. The map shows an inexplicable diagonal band of absence crossing SJ36, 46, 47 and 58. Sufficient survey work will probably show the species in almost all suitable waters and it is easy to prove breeding. There are records from the most easterly and westerly tetrads. In the east it is found in ponds at Coalhurst (98V) in the Pennines and in the west at Thurstaston (28G) on the Wirral. Other habitat types are represented by large lakes such as Warmingham Flash (76A), bogs such as Wybunbury Moss (65V), canals including both the Shropshire Union and Trent and Mersey and both the Rivers Dee and Weaver.

One of the earliest records was the 5th May 1990 at Broken Cross (87W) from D.Kitching and the latest to date is 12th September 1982 at Westlow (86M) from A.Savage.

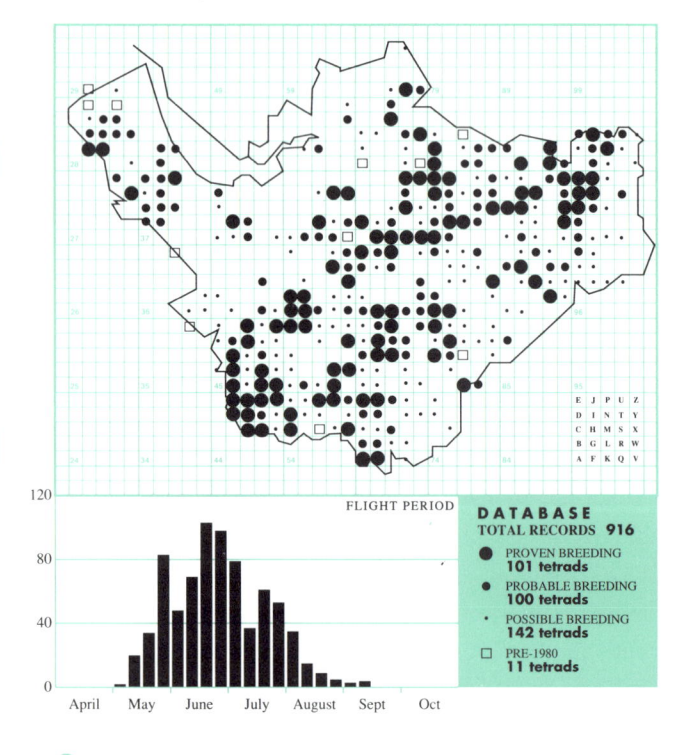

DATABASE
TOTAL RECORDS 916
● PROVEN BREEDING 101 tetrads
● PROBABLE BREEDING 100 tetrads
· POSSIBLE BREEDING 142 tetrads
□ PRE-1980 11 tetrads

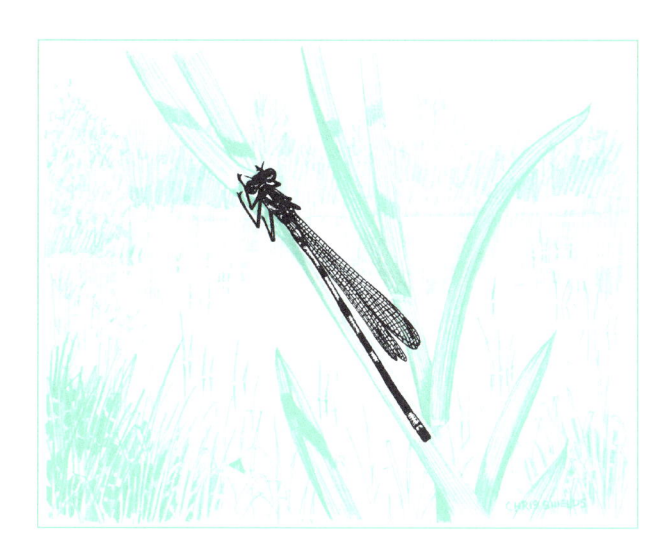

VARIABLE DAMSELFLY
Coenagrion pulchellum
(Vander Linden, 1825)

FIELD NOTES

Much of the comment relating to the Azure Damselfly (*Coenagrion puella*) is equally applicable to the Variable Damselfly. It is quite prepared to fly across water in bright sunshine although it is often found perched in the edge vegetation. It disperses quite widely.

CHESHIRE STATUS AND DISTRIBUTION

One distinction with regard to the preferred habitat of the Variable Damselfly is said to be a need for extensive vegetation and little open water. Shallow ponds, fens, watermeadows, marshes and ditches are all mentioned in the literature. It will also breed in slow flowing dykes and canals if these are well vegetated. It is clear that the specific habitat requirements are far more stringent than for the Azure Damselfly as there are many apparently ideal sites where only the more common species is present.

This is a scarce damselfly in Cheshire and, as it is declining nationally, it is a particularly important species. At the few sites in the county where it has been found it can, however, appear to outnumber the Azure Damselfly on some days of their joint flight period.

The Variable Damselfly was refound at Hatchmere (57L) in 1983 after there had been no records in Cheshire for 30 years. This was the result of detective work by S.Judd of Liverpool Museum, who had noticed specimens of this species from the Wirral in the museum's collection and searched for this species there and elsewhere in Cheshire. B.Walker also simultaneously recorded the species at Hatchmere (57L) and then at a series of marl pits in the Tiverton area (56F) during July 1985. Further searches in the surrounding area revealed more marl pit sites at Tarporley (56G) and Huxley (56A). The only other confirmed sites are the marl pit complex at Churton (45I) where the Variable Damselfly was discovered by R.Whitehead on 2nd July 1988 whilst searching for the Ruddy Darter (*Sympetrum sanguineum*) at ponds in the adjacent parish of Kings Marsh (45H).

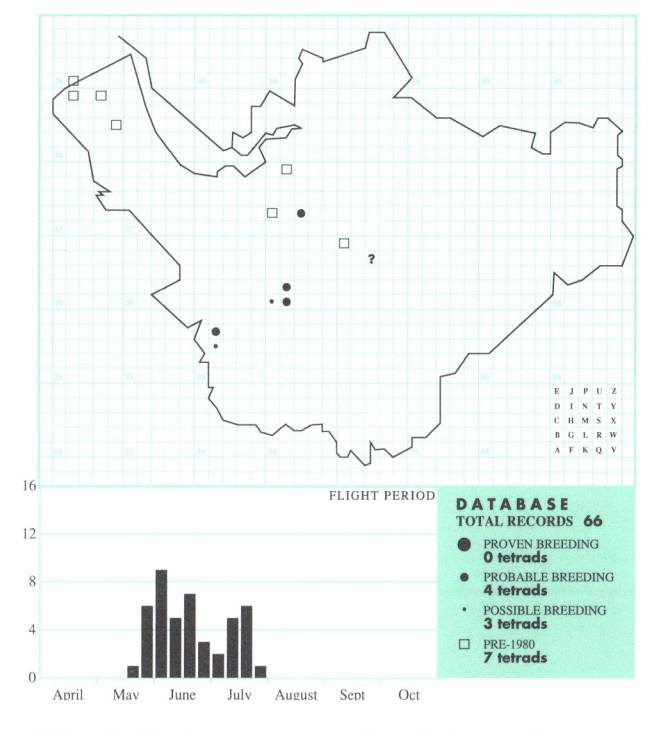

DATABASE
TOTAL RECORDS 66
- PROVEN BREEDING 0 tetrads
- PROBABLE BREEDING 4 tetrads
- POSSIBLE BREEDING 3 tetrads
- PRE-1980 7 tetrads

Historically there were a number of sites on the Wirral where this species could be found during the middle years of this century. W.K. Ford collected specimens at Meols (28J) in 1939, 1947 and 1950 which are now in the collection at Liverpool

Museum. Nearby, W.Rankin recorded specimens at Upton (28U) in 1952 and Landican (28X) in 1954. Regrettably these sites have now been filled in or greatly altered and the Variable Damselfly now appears to be absent on the Wirral. The only other pre-1980 record outside the Delamere area is from Frodsham (57J) by L.Greening in 1892 (Warrington Museum specimen).

The earliest record is 17th May 1952 at Upton (46E) or more recently 31st May 1987 at Hatchmere (57L) by R.Merritt and P.Adams. The latest sighting is also from Hatchmere (57L) on 27th July 1988 recorded by D.Jeffers.

'UNCORROBORATED' SPECIES RECORDS

One further species of damselfly (Zygoptera) has been thought to occur in the county during the present Tetrad Recording Scheme.

SCARCE BLUE-TAILED DAMSELFLY
Ischnura pumilio
(Charpentier, 1825)

Although a colour transparency was taken of a mating pair the angle of the photograph made it difficult to see either the pterostigma or the blue on the abdominal segments of the male. The habitat at Woolston sludge beds included seepages so there seemed some possibility that this was an exceptional record. Searches by S.Kennedy later in 1986 and over an extended area in 1987 failed to confirm the species.

26th July 1986   68P   R.Baguley
Woolston Eyes

CHAPTER FIVE
HABITATS & PRIME SITES

In the first chapter mention was made of the four broad categories of habitat, namely meres and larger waters, mosses and bogs, marl pits and smaller ponds, and rivers and streams. These are described in more detail in this chapter with the species of dragonfly likely to be found being tabulated and one prime site in each habitat being chosen for further description. IT MUST BE STRESSED THAT MENTION OF PARTICULAR WATERS IN NO WAY INDICATES A RIGHT OF PUBLIC ACCESS. CERTAIN KEY SITES ARE TOTALLY PRIVATE, WHILST OTHERS ARE EXTREMELY FRAGILE. SUCH SITES ARE DULY NOTED.

Meres & Larger Waters

From a national standpoint the Cheshire and Shropshire meres are important freshwater bodies, but distinguishing between them and other natural waters requires some definition. Reynolds (1979) describes a mere as: 'a small potentially fertile lake occupying a hollow in glacial drift deposits and maintained principally by ground flow water'. There are said to be more than 60 such meres of 1 hectare or over throughout the two counties.

A number of explanations have been put forward for the origin of the meres and most of these are associated with the melting of the ice sheet. One basic theory is that our present day meres are the waters which remain from originally much larger expanses trapped by the moraine deposits. Whilst this is not entirely discounted, it is thought that such shallower waters are more likely to have evolved into raised bogs, a habitat which is considered in the next section.

A more certain origin for some of the meres was as water remaining in hollows along which the main meltwater streams had flowed. As the ice sheet receded the force of these main streams became lessened by side streams, with debris gradually building up to trap standing water in a linked series of meres. This is more evident further south in the Plain although groups of meres in Cheshire are obviously associated with deposits from the end of the glaciation. A third source of some of our meres is kettle holes. These occurred when large blocks of the ice sheet became detached and isolated and gradually sank, eventually being buried by debris. Deep holes, created as these massive blocks melted, are now a feature of the Delamere area. A few meres have deep centres and wide shallow margins suggesting dual origins. Finally, mention was made in the introduction to the natural dissolving of underground salt deposits. Some of the Cheshire meres such as Budworth Mere and Pick Mere are almost certainly a result of this form of natural subsidence. Taxmere and Redesmere are also thought to have a similar origin whilst Melchett Mere at Tatton Park only formed during the 1920's due to natural brine subsidence. Rostherne Mere is much deeper than adjacent meres and this may be due to the original glacial mere becoming subsequently deeper due to subterranean salt dissolution.

Distribution of Meres & Larger Waters

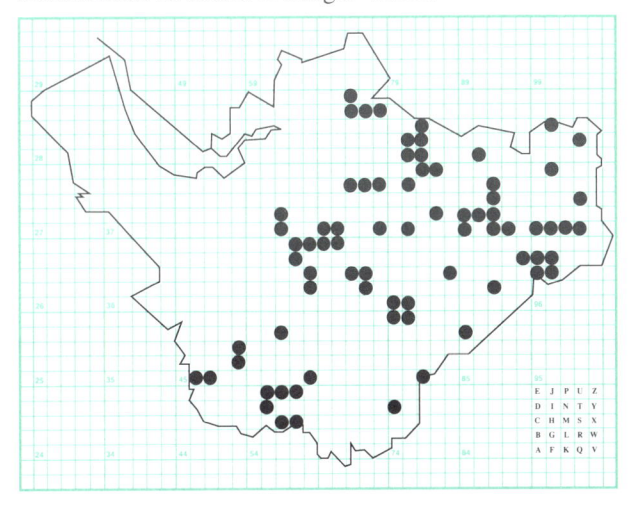

TABLE ONE

Species recorded on meres & large waters

Site	Grid	Aeshna cyanea	Aeshna juncea	Aeshna grandis	Anax imperator	Brachytron pratense	Cordulia aenea	Orthetrum cancellatum	Libellula depressa	Libellula quadrimaculata	Libellula fulva	Leucorrhinia dubia	Sympetrum danae	Sympetrum striolatum	Calopteryx splendens	Lestes sponsa	Erythromma najas	Pyrrhosoma nymphula	Ischnura elegans	Enallagma cyathigerum	Coenagrion puella	Coenagrion pulchellum
Astbury Mere	86L			●										•					•	●		
Astle Pool	87B			•															•	●		
Baddiley Mere	54Z/55V			•										•				•	•	●		
Barmere	54I/J																	•	•	•	•	
Balterley Mere	75K			●													•		●	•	•	
Belmont Hall Lake	67P			•														•		●		
Billinge Green Flash	67V			•	?	•			•	●				•			●	•	●	●	●	
Black Lake	88F	•	•	●	•			?		●		•	●	•					•	●		
Booths Mere	77U																	•				
Bosley Reservoir	96C/D/H/I																	•	•			
Bottom Flash	66M/S																	•	•			
Bottoms Reservoir	97K																	•				
Brereton Heath Lake	76X		•	•						•							•	•	●	•		
Capesthorne Lakes	87L																	•				
Combermere	54X	•																●		●	●	
Deer Park Mere	55F/K																	•		•		
Doddington Pool	74D																		•			
Forge Pool	67S/T			•						•				•					●		•	
Fourways & Delamere Sand Quarries	56U												•				•					
Gull Pool	56Z/66E		●	•	?	•	●			●			●	•			●	●	●	●	●	
Hassall Pool	75T			•														•	•			
Hatchmere	57L	●	●	●		●												●	●	●	●	•
Lawton Pool	85H			•														•				
Little Budworth Pool	56X																	•	•			
Lymm Dam	68T/Y			•										•					•	•		
Marbury Big Mere	54M																	•		•		
Marbury Small Mere	54S																	•		•		
Melchett Mere	78K			●						•							•		●	●		
Mere Mere	78F																	•		•		
New Pool	66J		•	•									●	•	●	•					•	
Norbury Mere	54P																				●	
Nunsmere	56Z		•	•					•		•					•		•	•	•		
Oakmere	56T/U									●			•	•					●	●	●	
Oulton Park Lake	56W/X																•		•			
Peckforton Mere	55N									•												
Peover Hall Lake	77R			•						•			•				•		●	•	●	
Petty Pool	66E/J/67A																•		●			
Pickmere	67T/Y																		•			
Poynton Pool	98H			●															•			
Quoisley Meres	54M			•																		
Radnor Mere	87M																					
Redesmere	87K			•																		
Rode Pool	85D																		•			
Rookery Pool	67F																	•	•		●	
Round Pool	56Z					•			●					●						•		
Rostherne Mere	78L/M	•	•	•					•	?			•	•			•		•	●		
Sandbach Flashes	76F																		•	•		
Styperson Pool	97J			•																•		
Sutton Reservoir	97A/F																		•	•		
Tabley Mere	77I													•			•		•			
Tatton Mere	77P/78K	•		•					•				•	•			●		●	●		
Taxmere	76R/W			●									•						•			
The Mere	37B	•		•															●		•	
Thornycroft Pools	87Q			●															•	•		
Trentabank Reservoir	97Q	•		•														•	•			
Warmingham Flash	76A																		●		●	
Windyhowe Pool	57K																	•	•	•		
Woolston Eyes	68P	●		•						•								•	●	●		

Key to symbols used   ● Proven breeding   ● Probable breeding   • Possible breeding   ? Uncorroborated record

The shallower flashes are due to relatively recent brine pumping and these are concentrated around Winsford, Nantwich and Sandbach. The table on page 52 lists most of the meres and larger waters by tetrad designation and shows all the dragonfly species found at each site to date.

Prime Site Profile
HATCHMERE SJ553722 (57L)

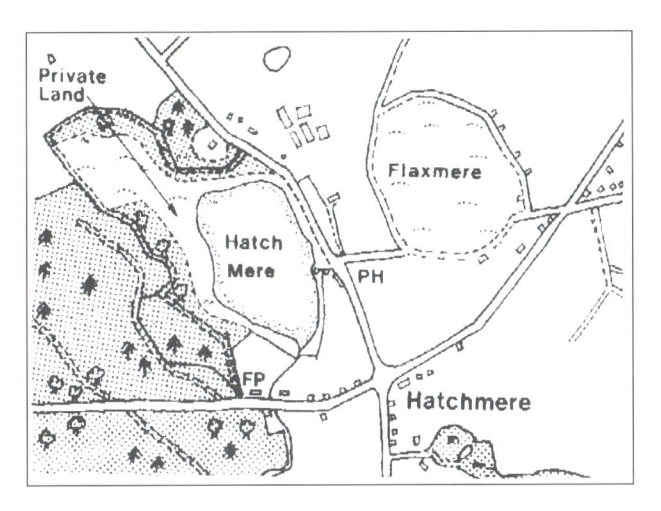

NOTE: HATCHMERE IS PRIVATE PROPERTY AND VISITORS MUST NOT STRAY FROM THE ROAD OR FOOTPATH. IT CANNOT BE EMPHASISED TOO STRONGLY THAT THE EDGE OF THE WATER IS FRAGILE HABITAT AND POTENTIALLY DANGEROUS IN PLACES.

At first sight Hatchmere might seem little different from many other apparently similar water bodies but in fact it provides a diverse range of freshwater habitats and is an outstanding site supporting 14 species of Odonata.

It is a medium sized mere situated on the northern edge of Delamere Forest near to the junction of the B5393 and B5152 roads. The eastern edge runs close to the latter road which provides a convenient car park for the summer bathers and as a consequence has the least vegetation. Here the mere has a sandy substratum with low concentrations of organic matter particularly in the open water. Moving around the northern side of the mere there are fine stands of Reed (*Phragmites australis*) and Lesser Reedmace (*Typha angustifolia*). These curve through the north-western corner to the western bank where there is the most diverse vegetation. This changes from floating peat bog at the edge, to carr further inland. The surface of the bog contains much Soft Rush (*Juncus effusus*), Marsh Pennywort (*Hydrocotyle vulgaris*), Marsh Cinquefoil (*Potentilla palustris*) and Gipsywort (*Lycopus europaeus*) and the water is highly organic. The carr comprises mainly Alder (*Alnus glutinosa*), Silver Birch (*Betula pendula*) and Oak (*Quercus robur*). Ground cover in the more open areas of the carr is dominated by Tufted Hair Grass (*Deschampsia cespitosa*) and Bracken (*Pteridium aquilinum*), together with occasional bushes of Hawthorn (*Craetaegus monogyna*) and Bog Myrtle (*Myrica gale*). Also of note in the water on the western side of the mere are sizeable areas of both White Water Lily (*Nymphaea alba*) and Yellow Water Lily (*Nuphar lutea*) whose leaves and flowers rise to the surface during the summer months.

So, on fine summer days what are the species of dragonfly which may be found in the Hatchmere area? Three species can be described as having particular importance, the first two because of their relative scarcity in the county and the third with regard to its abundance when compared with other sites.

The re-discovery of the Hairy Dragonfly (*Brachytron pratense*) at Hatchmere after many years was a milestone in the early days of the Tetrad Breeding Survey. This species is best looked for along the edge of the reeds on sunny days in early June when males may be seen searching for females. In a similar way the re-finding of the Variable Damselfly (*Coenagrion pulchellum*) at Hatchmere proved to be a considerable incentive for further searches. This species, as with the Hairy Dragonfly, appears to be declining nationally which makes it doubly important. It is most likely to be observed along the path around the western side of the mere. The third species is more difficult to see at close quarters, but anyone looking out onto the lily pads later in the summer will almost certainly prove successful in locating the Red-eyed Damselfly (*Erythromma najas*), which occurs here in substantial numbers.

Mosses & Bogs

This second main type of dragonfly habitat is closely linked with the meres, although in some respects the best preserved Cheshire mosses are of greater importance to a number of the scarcer species in the county. Reynolds (1979) has described the mosses as 'more or less closed peat filled hollows in the drift surface' and it will be seen that the mossland sites are very much like those occupied by some of the meres, with the two types of habitat often being closely associated. Indeed deposits of mud lying under the peat of the mosses are known to be similar to those at the bottom of present day meres, clear evidence, therefore, that the mosses have evolved through the gradual encroachment of edge vegetation across originally shallow waters. Initial plant growth usually comprises Reed (*Phragmites australis*) but sedges, and trees such as Alder (*Alnus glutinosa*), Birch (*Betula pendula*) and Pine (*Pinus sylvestris*), also start to grow once the open water becomes covered. This in turn encourages the growth of sphagnum (mainly *Sphagnum recurvum*) on the surface so that eventually peat from reeds, sedges and trees becomes overlain with moss peat. Where this occurs, with the moss taking up moisture from peat lying above the normal water table, it is described as a raised bog or hochmoor. Another type of moss is formed in some deeper and more steeply sided basins. Here rafts of sphagnum (mainly *Sphagnum cuspidatum*) decay and settle, with further growth occurring to create successive layers which eventually became a blanket floating directly upon the water. This type of moss is appropriately termed a quaking bog, or schwingmoor. It must be emphasised that, apart from the obvious dangers of walking on this second form of bog, it is an extremely fragile habitat which is easily destroyed by trampling.

The rate at which the different stages in the development of the moss take place, or even regress with the reeds again growing over the moss peat, is dependent upon the level of the water table relative to the surface of the bog. It is clear that complete infilling across the open mere can take place relatively quickly and certainly in less than a hundred years. An elderly resident of the Hatchmere area told us that he could remember clear water in Flaxmere (57L). The original shallow meres were probably soon overgrown during past drier periods, with layers of moss peat developing in wetter times. Mosses also grew over the surface of open water on the smaller and deeper meres but the largest of these meres resisted encroachment and remain today as highly rich and eutrophic lakes. The remaining mosses in Cheshire are part of a previously much more extensive series which includes those associated with the Mersey Valley. All these sites have been affected to a greater or lesser extent by peat digging which is carried out today mainly for horticultural purposes. This practice is currently the subject of much criticism from conservationists and considerable efforts are being made to save what is left of the mosses through the development of peat substitutes. Drainage for agricultural use, growth of secondary woodland, the more recent planting of conifers and even refuse disposal have also substantially reduced the original mosslands. There are many 'moss' names on the maps of Cheshire but the majority of the actual mosses have long since disappeared for these reasons.

The table on page 55 details the main areas in Cheshire with remaining mosses and bogs, although it must be remembered that only parts of the sites mentioned may prove suitable dragonfly habitat and not all are open to public access.

Distribution of Mosses & Bogs

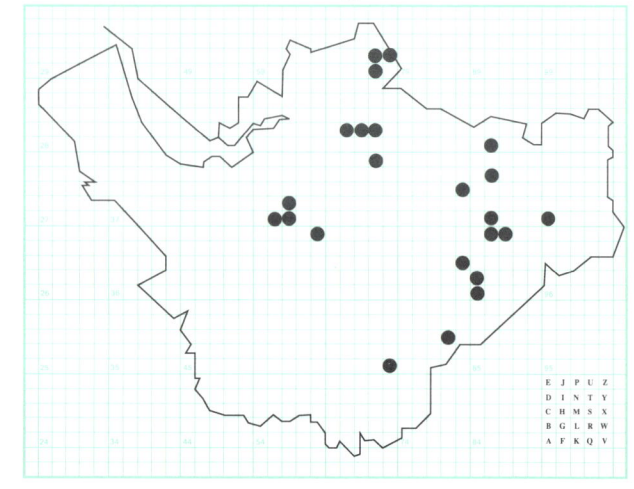

TABLE TWO

Species recorded in mosses & bogs

		Aeshna cyanea	*Aeshna juncea*	*Aeshna grandis*	*Anax imperator*	*Cordulia aenea*	*Orthetrum coerulescens*	*Libellula depressa*	*Libellula quadrimaculata*	*Leucorrhinia dubia*	*Sympetrum danae*	*Sympetrum striolatum*	*Calopteryx splendens*	*Calopteryx virgo*	*Lestes sponsa*	*Erythromma najas*	*Pyrrhosoma nymphula*	*Ischnura elegans*	*Enallagma cyathigerum*	*Coenagrion puella*
Arley Moss	67U				•				•									•	•	●
Bagmere	76X		•						•				•				•	●	•	●
Black Lake	57F	●	●	●				●	●	●	●	●			•		●	●	•	●
Blakemere	57K			•					•		•	•					●		•	●
Brookhouse Moss	86A/B	•		•							•						●			
Danes Moss	97A	●	•	•					•		●	•			●		●	•	•	•
Flaxmere	57L	•		•					•		●	•					●			
Lindow Moss	88F	•	•	•					•		●	•					●			
Lower Moss Wood	77X	●	●	●	•				●		●	•	●				●	•	•	•
Risley Moss	69Q/R	●	●	●			•		●		●	●			•		●	●	●	●
Shemmy Moss/Abbots Moss/Lily Pool	56Z		•	●		•		•	●	●	●			•			●		●	●
Wybunbury Moss	65V	•		•					•								●			

Key to symbols used ● Proven breeding • Probable breeding · Possible breeding

Prime Site Profile
Risley Moss SJ665918 (69Q/R)

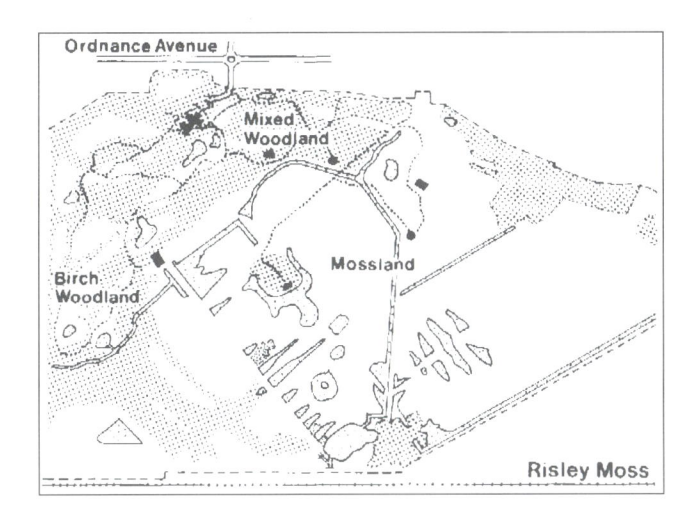

The choice of Risley Moss for our prime site is fortunate as the whole of the moss was situated in Lancashire prior to the county boundary changes. Entrance to the site is from Ordnance Avenue in Birchwood, Warrington New Town. Risley has been surveyed more thoroughly than many of the other mosses with reports being written by Dawson (1981) and Taylor (1983).

Risley Moss is an excellent example of a raised bog system and much peat remains despite the removal of a complete layer by the British Peat Moss Litter Company during a period of almost sixty years from 1870. Originally the peat was thickest at the centre and formed a characteristic dome shape, but drainage through channels dug to lower the water table in order to effectively strip the peat has had the most significant effect upon the moss. Although the water level has been raised over recent years to encourage renewal of the bog, dry surface conditions for many years have led to the almost complete coverage by Purple Moor Grass (*Molinia caerulea*) and Heather (*Calluna vulgaris*) in the open moss. Wetter areas are largely covered with Cottongrass species (*Eriophorum angustifolium* and *E. vaginatum*) together with other wetland species including Cross-leaved Heath (*Erica tetralix*), Cranberry (*Vaccinium oxycoccus*) and some sphagnum species.

The area of the moss designated as a Site of Special Scientific Interest (S.S.S.I) comprises 85 hectares with an additional area still in private ownership. Management of the reserve over the past fifteen years has been geared to returning as much of the area as possible to natural mossland. This has mainly been achieved by raising the water level, using sluices to control the flow, and so creating more open water. The woodland area pools have been formed by clearing trees from around hollows which were then deepened and lined. On the moss itself new pools have also been dug in addition to the long water-filled channels left after the peat digging. The map on page 55 shows the main areas of interest for dragonflies. A typical mossland pool at Risley has relatively acid water at pH 4.5 with marginal vegetation which includes Soft Rush (*Juncus effusus*), Jointed Rush (*Juncus articulatus*), Common Cotton Grass (*Eriophorum angustifolium*), Harestail Cotton Grass (*Eriophorum vaginatum*) and Purple Moor Grass (*Molinia caerulea*). The maximum number of dragonfly species recorded by Taylor (1983) as either being on territory or egg-laying on a mossland pool was ten. Six Anisoptera (dragonflies) were noted; Brown Hawker (*Aeshna grandis*), Southern Hawker (*Aeshna cyanea*), Common Hawker (*Aeshna juncea*), Four-spotted Chaser (*Libellula quadrimaculata*), Common Darter (*Sympetrum striolatum*) and the Black Darter (*Sympetrum danae*) plus four Zygoptera (damselflies); Common Blue Damselfly (*Enallagma cyathigerum*), Azure Damselfly (*Coenagrion puella*), Blue-tailed Damselfly (*Ischnura elegans*) and the Large Red Damselfly (*Pyrrhosoma nymphula*).

The best of the woodland pools studied also had the lowest pH value at 5.0 with the vegetation differing by having Greater Reedmace (*Typha latifolia*) at the edge plus Duckweed (*Lemna* sp.) and Pondweed (*Potomageton sp.*) as surface vegetation. The variety of dragonfly at the woodland site was similar with ten species being recorded. Compared with the mossland the Four-spotted Chaser was not seen but the Emerald Damselfly (*Lestes sponsa*) was an additional species. Fourteen species of dragonfly have been recorded from the site of which three may be described as vagrants, namely the Keeled Skimmer (*Orthetrum coerulescens*), the Emperor Dragonfly (*Anax imperator*) and the Banded Demoiselle (*Calopteryx splendens*).

Shemmy Moss SJ596685 (56Z)
Abbots Moss SJ598687 (56Z)

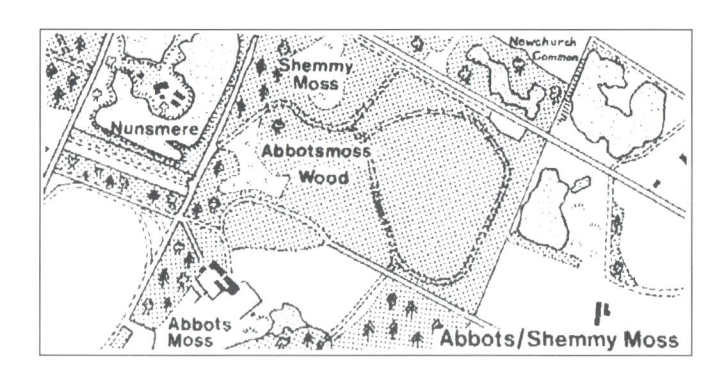

NOTE: BOTH SITES ARE PRIVATE AND THE MOSSES ARE FRAGILE AND DANGEROUS HABITATS.

Although the raised bog at Risley was chosen as the main site to cover in this section these two further mosses are worthy of particular mention. They are excellent examples of quaking bogs and are the breeding sites for two further Cheshire dragonflies. These bogs, together with the adjacent Gull Pool, are the stronghold for the White-faced Darter (*Leucorrhinia dubia*) in the county and the high numbers of this species which occur here make Shemmy Moss and Abbots Moss the most southerly key sites for this species. Whilst the Downy Emerald (*Cordulia aenea*) can be found more commonly elsewhere in the country, the area including these mosses contains the only known breeding sites for this species in Cheshire. These two species can be seen very well however in the rides of the surrounding woodland, particularly in the post emergence period. A further excellent site for viewing the White-faced Darter is Black Lake SJ537709 (57F) which is owned by the Forestry Commission and managed as a reserve by the Cheshire Conservation Trust.

Marl Pits & Smaller Ponds

Marl pits and small ponds form a third main category of habitat and these are probably of greater significance for dragonflies in Cheshire than in any similar area of England as there are still more ponds here than in any other English county. The Cheshire Conservation Trust has estimated a figure of 86,000, or over 25% of all English ponds, with as many in some 1 kilometre squares as in the whole of some other counties. Even allowing for the much more rapid rate of loss over recent years, any exploration of the county will show just how many remain. So, once again, why is it that Cheshire is fortunate in having such an abundance of yet another excellent dragonfly habitat?

The glacial deposits in the Plain were mentioned in the introduction to this chapter and these deposits occur in the form of till which frequently contains a band of clay lying a few feet below the surface. Leaching by rainwater and continual cropping had the effect of increasing soil acidity and reducing yields until the presence of calcium carbonate was discovered in the clay. This provided a counteraction to the acidity and had the effect of restoring fertility. Digging out the clay (marl) and spreading it over the surrounding field was termed 'marling' and from this the name marl pit was derived.

The history of marling suggests that pit digging was being carried out as early as the 14th century. Reference was made by Leland in Hewitt (1919) that the likely origin of the *"manifolde pooles and lakes in Chestershire was by diggings of marle for fattynge the barren ground there to beare good corne"*. The size of the pit was determined by the area over which the extracted marl was to be laid. As much as 100 tons per acre were spread, with a pit for a 2 hectare field measuring 18 metres by 11 metres, having been dug to a depth of almost 3 metres. In Cheshire there are still pits of a much larger size. The marl was taken out by cart and consequently the pits often have one shallow sloping side. Even during digging they would frequently fill with water due to striking springs. At least one pit per field was dug, although in Cheshire there are often multiple pits. Two and three were dug adjacent to each other with the trios often forming a cloverleaf shape. Many marl pits and small ponds have deteriorated or disappeared over recent years for several reasons. Change in land use has meant that ponds have been filled in by farmers, some with refuse or tyres, nitrogen fertiliser run-off has ruined others through enrichment, and a general lowering of the water-table has meant many ponds have become totally overgrown or have dried-up altogether. The discovery of a considerable number of such degraded ponds has been one of the frequent disappointments of our survey. Loss of individual ponds may impoverish the dragonfly population of a much wider area because remaining healthy but scattered ponds may not be adequate to support viable populations of all species.

Characteristics of marl pits described in studies of their flora also appear to have some influence upon the occurrence of dragonflies. Some species of dragonfly seem to be associated with the presence of particular types of emergent/floating vegetation, or with certain marginal plants. Attempts have been made recently to assess marl pits using a value ranking system for the different species of plant found at a particular pond. A high total score for a wide species diversity may well also be a very useful indicator for dragonflies. The presence of some of the uncommon and high scoring plants such as Trifid Bur Marigold (*Bidens tripartita*), Frogbit (*Hydrocharis morsus-ranae*), Purple Loosestrife (*Lythrum salicaria*) or Water Milfoil (*Myriophyllum* sp.) may be of less importance to dragonflies than some low-scoring common plants such as Common Water Plantain (*Alisma plantago-aquatica*), Soft Rush (*Juncus effusus*) or Broad-leaved Pondweed (*Potomageton natans*).

The degree of shading is obviously important as ponds which are heavily shaded support the least variety of plants and in keeping with our findings the least number, if any, of dragonfly species. Where fences have remained trees have been able to grow up around the pond, so gradually reducing its habitat value. Perhaps the oldest ponds are amongst those most completely shaded due to being fenced in the past. It became very easy for us to assess from a distance those ponds which would have little potential for dragonflies according to the extent of the cover. The presence of some trees and bushes around the pond edge is of benefit to dragonflies however, particularly if they are growing around the northern and eastern edges.

The most likely conditions for a high number of dragonfly species to breed in ponds are:

1. Moderate size with some trees or bushes on the northern or eastern sides to provide shelter for damselflies on windy but sunny days, and roosting sites for dragonflies at night.
2. High diversity of marginal and emergent vegetation with a sizeable proportion of open water.
3. A neutral to alkaline pH and low levels of dissolved nitrates.
4. Some considerable age with near proximity to other waters containing good breeding populations of dragonflies.

There have been a number of dragonfly surprises during our survey of Cheshire's ponds. One species, the Ruddy Darter (*Sympetrum sanguineum*) at the northern limit of its main national distribution has been discovered for the first time breeding in marl pits in the south-west of the county. The Red-eyed Damselfly (*Erythromma najas*) has been found at many more sites than would have been imagined several years ago, with quite small ponds being used for breeding where the requisite floating plants were growing. The nationally declining Variable Damselfly (*Coenagrion pulchellum*) has also been found in a limited number of marl pits. Without question there is much more to be discovered as only a relatively small proportion of the county's ponds have been visited. The large number of individual ponds makes it inappropriate to list particular sites as in the previous habitat sections.

Prime Site Profile
CHURTON MARL PITS
SJ430565 (45I)

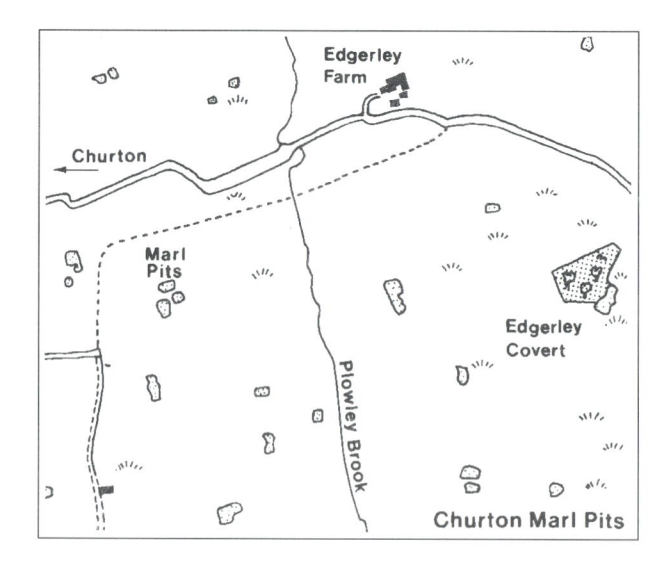

NOTE: THESE MARL PITS LIE ON PRIVATE LAND BUT CAN BE CLEARLY VIEWED FROM THE ADJACENT PUBLIC FOOTPATH. ON NO ACCOUNT SHOULD ATTEMPTS BE MADE TO APPROACH THE WATER BY LEAVING THE PATH.

The selection of one site from so many excellent ponds in the county has again been difficult. This particular cluster of marl pits however exemplifies most of the ideal characteristics described above. Perhaps the only aspect which appears to be lacking is that of shelter on the northerly side although the ponds were dug quite deeply and there is some Crack Willow (*Salix fragilis*) between the pits, with hedgerows and coppice a short distance away. Modern fencing and some tree planting will ensure a further improvement in sheltering. The pits can be seen to have been dug as a trio in a cloverleaf formation. At the water's edge Greater Reedmace (*Typha latifolia*), Soft Rush (*Juncus effusus*), Yellow Flag (*Iris pseudacorus*), Lesser Water Parsnip (*Berula erecta*) and Greater Birdsfoot Trefoil (*Lotus uliginosus*) are profuse. Within the ponds Yellow Water-Lily (*Nuphar lutea*), the uncommon Fringed Water-Lily (*Nymphoides peltata*), Frogbit (*Hydrocharis morsus-ranae*) and

Broad-leaved Pondweed (*Potomageton natans*) contribute to a midsummer picture which would be difficult to beat anywhere in the country.

Our attention was drawn to the marl pits in the Churton area after reports of photographs of a dragonfly originally thought to be the Common Darter (*Sympetrum striolatum*) but which was subsequently positively identified as the Ruddy Darter (*Sympetrum sanguineum*). Further searches have also revealed the presence of the Variable Damselfly (*Coenagrion pulchellum*) and with so few sites in the county for this important species these ponds have proven to be of even greater importance. The dragonflies found so far at the Churton marl pits are listed in table 3 below. It should be noted that two further species could well be expected, namely the Southern Hawker (*Aeshna cyanea*) and the Common Darter (*Sympetrum striolatum*).

TABLE THREE

Species recorded at Churton marl pits

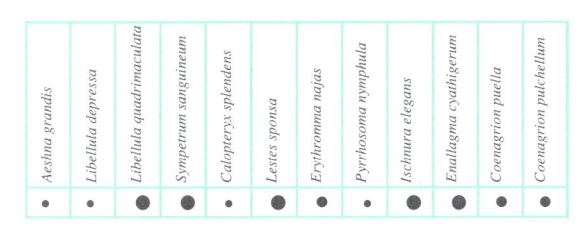

Species	Status
Aeshna grandis	Possible breeding
Libellula depressa	Possible breeding
Libellula quadrimaculata	Proven breeding
Sympetrum sanguineum	Proven breeding
Calopteryx splendens	Possible breeding
Lestes sponsa	Proven breeding
Erythromma najas	Probable breeding
Pyrrhosoma nymphula	Probable breeding
Ischnura elegans	Proven breeding
Enallagma cyathigerum	Proven breeding
Coenagrion puella	Probable breeding
Coenagrion pulchellum	Probable breeding

Key to symbols used:
- ● Proven breeding
- ● Probable breeding
- • Possible breeding

Rivers, Streams & Canals

Anyone giving cursory consideration to the rivers and canals feeding the Mersey Basin could be excused for imagining them to have little potential for dragonflies. Whilst it is certainly true that the Mersey itself is largely biologically dead, many of the other watercourses feeding it provide extensive stretches with suitable habitat for a wide range of Odonata. These include certain specialist species which require flowing water to breed successfully. In addition, the Dee has proved to be a particularly important habitat as it is subject to less industrial pollution than the other main Cheshire rivers. The majority of Cheshire's rivers have their source in the Pennine uplands of Derbyshire, Staffordshire and Greater Manchester. From the peat bogs of the hills they flow westwards, often following a rocky course, until they reach the Cheshire Plain whence they become much slower, muddier and often meandering. Two rivers, the Gowy and the Weaver, rise in the Plain below the Peckforton hills and pass within half a mile of each other in different directions. Whilst the Gowy takes a direct course northwards to the Mersey at Stanlow the Weaver flows south and east to Audlem before finally turning northwards. Second only to the Mersey is the Dee which rises many miles away in the uplands of Gwynedd and flows eastwards into Cheshire on a course that was originally fed by the Severn before glaciation caused the latter river to change course to the south. Canals, as dragonfly habitat, might be considered to be still water features similar to ponds but they also have some similarities to rivers in that they are linear. Whilst they are not necessarily suitable habitat for specialist river dwelling species they do provide routeways along which migration has been observed on a number of occasions during the present survey. Some canals are used to supply water for both domestic and industrial use and the flows generated can be the equivalent of natural watercourses. A good example of this is the Llangollen Canal which is fed from the Dee above the Horseshoe Falls in Llangollen and carries drinking water to Hurlestone near Nantwich. There are over 120 miles of canal in Cheshire. (The disused St Helens Canal, in places, also provides habitat similar to ponds and marl pits). On rivers the greatest number of dragonfly species is generally found where there are plenty of slow, clear and calm areas particularly where there is also abundant marginal vegetation. These conditions are similar to those found in marl pits and ponds and it is likely that similar species of Odonata will occur. However there are several species which are only found where there is a current of water and their requirements range from rocky torrents of hilly country to the steady flowing rivers of the lowlands.

Probably the greatest threat to rivers as a habitat is that of pollution. In a dynamic system such as a watercourse, the introduction of any pollutant is rapidly spread over a great distance with consequent disastrous effects on the fauna. Whilst the cause of the damage may be flushed out of the system quite quickly, its effects may last for many years as there is often no nearby habitat from which re-colonisation can take place. Historically many of the tributaries of the Mersey were destroyed as habitat for Odonata by industrial effluents, whereas the completely rural rivers, such as the Weaver above Nantwich, were unaffected. Unfortunately the situation has deteriorated due to intensification of farming practice and many formerly clean rivers are now suffering the effects of pollution by silage effluent, pesticides and slurry run-off. Additionally, nitrogen run-off over-enriches the water causing algal blooms, and sewage outfalls continue to reduce water quality to an extent that most species cannot survive.

In Cheshire only four specialist river dwelling Odonata have been definitely recorded. These are: the Club-tailed Dragonfly (*Gomphus vulgatissimus*), the Hairy Dragonfly (*Brachytron pratense*), the Banded Demoiselle (*Calopteryx splendens*) and the Beautiful Demoiselle (*Calopteryx virgo*).

It should be noted that whilst three of these species are known to breed only in flowing water in Cheshire, the Hairy Dragonfly also breeds in lakes. It is also suspected that the Common Hawker (*Aeshna juncea*) breeds in a number of slow sections on the upland streams in the east of the County. A further species is quite likely to be found within the County although no confirmed sighting has yet been made. This is the Golden-ringed Dragonfly (*Cordulegaster boltonii*) which is commonly found on fast flowing upland waters in the west of Britain.

The principal rivers and canals together with the species so far found on them are listed in the table below. It is apparent from this table that the rivers and streams have not been adequately researched for Odonata and this is particularly true in that there is no definitive evidence on the range of the Banded Demoiselle on the Weaver above Nantwich. The Gowy has had little attention paid to the possibility of the Club-tailed Dragonfly breeding on the marshland section above Stanlow. The lack of access to many riverbanks makes the task difficult but anyone making the effort to investigate the Odonata of the Cheshire rivers could well be rewarded with new discoveries.

TABLE FOUR

Species recorded on rivers, streams & canals

	Aeshna cyanea	*Aeshna juncea*	*Aeshna grandis*	*Brachytron pratense*	*Gomphus vulgatissimus*	*Libellula quadrimaculata*	*Sympetrum striolatum*	*Calopteryx splendens*	*Calopteryx virgo*	*Erythromma najas*	*Pyrrhosoma nymphula*	*Ischnura elegans*	*Enallagma cyathigerum*	*Coenagrion puella*
Bakestonedale Stream		•									•			
Bollinhurst Brook											•			
Cumberland Brook		•												
Dane			•					●						•
Dean								●			•	•	•	
Dee					●			●			•	•	•	
Gowy			•			•		•			•	•		
Llangollen Canal								●			•			
Macclesfield Canal								●			•			
Rostherne Mere Stream								●						
Shropshire Union Canal												•		•
St. Helens Canal			•			•						●		●
Tatton Mere Stream								●			•			
Weaver	•		•	●				●	●		●	●	•	●

Key to symbols used
● Proven breeding
● Probable breeding
• Possible breeding

Prime Site Profile
RIVER WEAVER, VALE ROYAL (66P/67F/K)

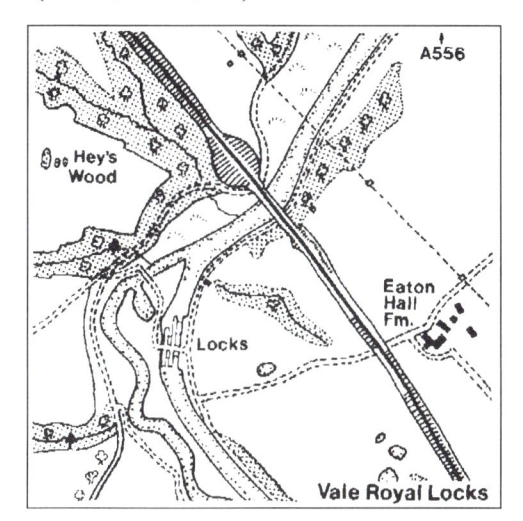

NOTE: ACCESS IS VIA A PATH ALONG THE EDGE OF THE RIVER WHICH IS USED BY THE PUBLIC AND FROM WHICH, IN EARLY JUNE, A GOOD VIEW CAN BE GAINED OF MOST OF THE SPECIES FOUND HERE.

The varying requirements of the different riverine species make it difficult to pick a typical river site. In terms of numbers of species and quantity of insects to be seen however, there can only be one choice, the River Weaver where it passes close to the site of Vale Royal Abbey. Ever since the Weaver was made navigable from the Mersey up to Winsford in the first half of the eighteenth century it has been subject to alteration and improvement for navigational purposes. Normally such works would lead to a reduction in the wildlife value of the river and this is certainly true of the canalised sections which tend to be straight and deep right to the banks which are usually steep and protected by stone or concrete. However the canalisation led to the bypassing of some loops leaving sections for weir streams which have retained a more 'natural' profile and which are undisturbed by boats.

At Vale Royal there is a long loop, of just over one kilometre in length, around the locks. Running from south-east to north-west, it is separated from the lock cut or channel by a narrow island. The river channel lies in a well sheltered position being some three metres lower than the lock cut. To the south and west of the river the banks are thickly wooded with a mixture of trees including Oak (*Quercus robur*), Ash (*Fraxinus excelsior*), Horse Chestnut (*Aesculus hippocastanum*), Lime (*Tilia x europaea*), Sycamore (*Acer pseudoplatanus*) and Silver Birch (*Betula pendula*). The banks support a number of Willow (*Salix* sp.) and Alder (*Alnus glutinosa*). The island is grazed by cattle and consequently the banks on the north and east side of the river channel support only a few trees. At the waters edge are found stands of Yellow Flag (*Iris pseudacorus*) and Reed (*Phragmites australis*) interspersed with Marsh Woundwort (*Stachys palustris*), Water Mint (*Mentha aquatica*), Watercress (*Nasturtium officinale*) and Water Forget-me-not (*Myosotis palustris*). On the water are found Flotegrass (*Glyceria fluitans*), White Water-lily (*Nymphaea alba*), Common and Large Duckweed (*Lemna minor* and *Lemna polyrhiza*) and Pondweed (*Potomageton* sp.).

The pollution problems of the Weaver below Winsford (there have been several major fish kills over the last few years) led to it being discounted as a possible important site for Odonata until a visit by D.Kitching during 1988 revealed the presence of the largest breeding colony of the Hairy Dragonfly (*Brachytron pratense*) in the county. Further study showed that this was also the only known river site for the Red-eyed Damselfly (*Erythromma najas*) which is present here in considerable numbers. The presence of these, and the other species listed on page 60, is not easy to explain on an often polluted river. The only hypothesis that we can offer at present is that the local conditions are such as to protect this short section of river by diverting pollutants along the lock cut. In summer there is a reduced flow on the river and very little water passes through the sluices at the head of this section as the main flow is handled by other sluices at the locks. Consequently, when the problems of pollution are least easily flushed away, the old river section at Vale Royal is partially protected. Additionally, if pollutants do enter this section the flow of water through the sluices will assist in oxygenating the water so possibly alleviating the problem.

REFERENCES

Arkle, J. (1898). Dragonflies in 1897. The Entomologist, 31: 33- 35.

Brian, A.D., Price, P.S., Redwood, B.C. & Wheeler, E. (1987). The flora of the marl pits (ponds) in one Cheshire parish. Watsonia, 16: 417-26.

Cooke, B. (1882). Contribution to a list of the Neuroptera (in the Linnaean sense) of Lancashire and Cheshire, the North of Lancaster excepted. Naturalist, p121.

Dawson, R. (1981). Dragonflies at Risley Moss Educational Nature Reserve, Warrington. Unpublished report for Risley Moss Ranger Service.

Ford, W.K. (1953). Lancashire and Cheshire Odonata (A preliminary list). North West Naturalist, 6: 227-233. New Series No.2.

Ford, W.K. (1954). Lancashire and Cheshire Odonata (Some further notes). North West Naturalist, 2: 602-603. New Series No.4.

Hammond, C.O. (1983). The Dragonflies of Great Britain and Ireland. Harley Books, Colchester.

Hewitt, W. (1919). Marl and marling in Cheshire. Proceedings of the Liverpool Geological Society, 13: 24-28.

Holland, H. (1808). A general view of the agriculture of Cheshire. Board of Agriculture.

Judd, S. (1986). The past and present status of the damselfly *Coenagrion pulchellum* (Van Der Linden) (Odonata: Coenagriidae) - In Cheshire and parts of it's adjacent counties, corresponding to the 100 Km Square SJ. (3 3). Entomologists' Record and Journal of Variation. 98: 57-61.

Lucas, W.J. (1900). British Dragonflies (Odonata). Upcott Gill, London.

Lucas, W.J. (1919). The Odonata of the Lancashire and Cheshire District. Lancashire and Cheshire Naturalist, 12: 23-27.

Lucas, W.J. (1930). Paranuroptera. In a checklist of the fauna of Lancashire and Cheshire Part 1. (Ed. Lawson, A.K.) p78. Lancashire and Cheshire Fauna Committee. T. Buncle and Co, Arbroath.

Reynolds, C.S. (1979). The limnology of the eutrophic meres of the Shropshire-Cheshire plain. Field Studies, 5: 93-173.

Savage, A.A. (1987). Hatchmere - A clue in the search for Sites of Special Scientific Interest. Cheshire Dragonflies - Annual Report, 1986: 31-33.

Taylor, G. (1983). Odonata, Risley Moss. Unpublished report for Risley Moss Ranger Service.